HEALING A MARRIAGE AFFLICTED BY PORNOGRAPHY

God's Opportunity

A WIFE'S PERSPECTIVE

Praise for God's Opportunity

This book elegantly captures the array of raw emotions, confusion, pain, and struggle women feel when navigating their husband's unwanted pornography viewing. As I read God's Opportunity, I thought of all the women and couples I have worked with over the years wishing each of them had a copy of this book to validate their tender experiences, provide insight into the complexities of this struggle, and to foster hope and vision for a healthy and helpful path forward. Elizabeth's journey is a remarkable testament of her perseverance through heartache, commitment to her covenants, and love of our Savior. God's Opportunity is a must-read for Latter-day Saints seeking to better navigate pornography concerns in an honest, balanced, and healing way.

Dr. Cameron Staley, Clinical Psychologist
author of *Confessions of an LDS Sex Researcher*

Most Latter-day Saints recognize that pornography is a serious challenge, but they don't always know good strategies for coping and overcoming it. Written from the perspective of a faithful and loving spouse, this book can help those who love someone struggling with pornography just as much as someone who is working to overcome it themselves.

Casey Paul Griffiths, author of
*The Scripture Central Commentary
on the Doctrine and Covenants*

This book pours hope from its pages. It has impacted my heart, offering a pattern of compassion to follow and reminding me that, no matter our trials, Christ's power can guide us every step of the way.

Neill F. Marriott, 2nd Counselor in the
Young Woman's General President from
2013-2018 and author of *Seek This Jesus*

HEALING A MARRIAGE AFFLICTED BY PORNOGRAPHY

God's Opportunity

A WIFE'S
PERSPECTIVE

ELIZABETH WELLS

CFI
An imprint of Cedar Fort, Inc.
Springville, Utah

© 2025 Elizabeth Wells
All rights reserved.

No part of this book may be reproduced in any form whatsoever, whether by graphic, visual, electronic, film, microfilm, tape recording, or any other means, without prior written permission of the publisher, except in the case of brief passages embodied in critical reviews and articles.

This is not an official publication of The Church of Jesus Christ of Latter-day Saints. The opinions and views expressed herein belong solely to the author and do not necessarily represent the opinions or views of Cedar Fort, Inc. Permission for the use of sources, graphics, and photos is also solely the responsibility of the author.

Paperback ISBN 13: 978-1-4621-4864-6
eBook ISBN 13: 978-1-4621-4865-3

Published by CFI, an imprint of Cedar Fort, Inc.
2373 W. 700 S., Suite 100, Springville, UT 84663
Distributed by Cedar Fort, Inc., www.cedarfort.com

Library of Congress Cataloging Number: 2024947515

Cover design by Shawnda Craig
Cover design © 2025 Cedar Fort, Inc.
Edited and Typeset by Liz Kazandzhy

Printed in the United States of America

10 9 8 7 6 5 4 3 2 1

Printed on acid-free paper

This book is dedicated to the man who kept his freckle promise. Thank you for never giving up on us, on yourself, or on the Lord, and for allowing me to share our story. Your quiet, humble strength is inspiring and so, so beautiful.

Contents

Introduction 1

Part 1: I Feel 9

   1   I Feel Like I'm Going Crazy 11

   2   I Feel Alone and Want to Hide 15

   3   I Have Trauma 17

   4   Underneath It All, I Feel Fear 23

Part 2: I Need 29

   5   I Need to Learn 31

   6   I Need the Book of Mormon 33

   7   I Need to Believe 43

   8   I Need Trust to Be Rebuilt 47

   9   I Need to Be Careful Too 51

  10   I Need to Heal 55

    11 I Need Support and Connection 61

Part 3: I Can 99

    12 I Can Let My Spouse Take Responsibility 101

    13 I Can Love My Spouse as Jesus Christ Loves Us 109

    14 I Can Face This Evil with My Spouse 125

    15 I Can See My Husband through God's Eyes 133

    16 I Can Keep My Covenants 139

    17 I Can Experience True Intimacy 147

    18 I Can Help Others 153

    19 I Can Be Humble 161

    20 I Can Come to Be Grateful for This Extremity 169

About the Author 176

Introduction

IMAGINE WALKING WITH YOUR HUSBAND DOWN A LONG ROAD. YOUR hand in his serves as a reminder that you both have promised before God, angels, and others that you will walk through life and death together. This is a beautiful walk.

Then you notice something—an object clutched tightly in his opposite hand, carefully concealed so no one else will see. Before you can fully make out what it is, you're suddenly thrown into a storm of fire and flying debris and you crash into the ground.

Everything around you goes quiet. Thick, suffocating smoke fills your lungs and you gasp for breath. As you scrape at the rubble to try to pull yourself up, you notice the blood, cuts, and pieces of shrapnel that cover your hands, your arms—your entire body.

Unfamiliar pain starts to set in as you begin to piece it together. An explosion has gone off, and the safest person in your life was holding the grenade.

You frantically look around and finally see your injured husband limping toward you. When he's within arm's reach, he slowly extends his hand out, looking down to avoid eye contact.

Battling competing emotions, you desperately want to simultaneously throw your arms around him—partly to support him and partly to have him support you—*and* scream out every question and thought plaguing you at that moment, no matter how it makes him feel.

Ultimately, for reasons you don't quite understand yet, you do neither. Instead, you simply reach out your bloody hand to meet his and silently keep walking, sensing another explosion just around the corner.

Now leave this scene on repeat. Let it play out over and over again. Not knowing how long it would go on, or at what frequency, would there come a time when you would stop reaching out to hold his hand? Maybe you'd resolve to keep walking next to him but keep your distance in preparation for the next explosion. Or would you want to stop walking with him altogether? What if there came a time when he became so injured that he could no longer limp over to you and reach out his hand? Would you go to him?

If you are the wife of a man who repeatedly views pornography, then this allegory and these questions probably sound all too familiar.

I have been on this very walk for many years. I wrote this book to let you know that you are not alone and that your walk can be a beautiful walk once again because of the gospel of Jesus Christ—and *sooner than you probably think.*

About Us

My name is Elizabeth Wells. My husband, Luke, and I were married and sealed for time and all eternity in the Columbia South Carolina Temple of The Church of Jesus Christ of Latter-day Saints.

Marriage agreed with us. Everything felt magical—that is, everything except for one thing.

Luke has struggled with pornography and masturbation since he was very young. What started as innocent curiosity turned into a habit he hated and that made him hate himself. I learned of this early on, so while our first years of marriage were sacred and wonderful, they were also terribly heartbreaking.

He was holding that grenade as we walked daily life together, and I never knew when or if he would pull the pin. I wasn't sure how to reconcile the internal and external conflict that the unknown created, but I knew I wanted to try to find a way.

About It

Oftentimes, unwanted and repeated pornography viewing is not really about sex. Rather, it's an unhealthy coping mechanism for uncomfortable or difficult emotions, such as shame, stress, arousal, and even boredom. It's an attempt to escape discomfort in the moment.

This is a trick of the adversary, though, based on a lie that the father of all lies has been using to confuse and lead astray the hearts of the children of men for millennia. There are many ways he tries to get us to escape when faced with the hard parts of mortality. One of those ways is through viewing pornography. He knows that the strong stimuli sex naturally provides is the perfect avenue for a reactionary escape.

While this escape may help to initially offer brief relief from current uncomfortable realities, the long-term effects are destructive. Those who turn to pornography disconnect from themselves, from those around them, and from God. Their self-esteem quickly crumbles to a sense of worthlessness as they struggle to see anything in themselves but *bad*.

A common misconception is that the secret life of unwanted pornography viewing is reserved for the over-sexualized, the weirdos, and the perverts. This is usually not the case. Being involved in this form of escape is more common than most of us probably realize, and it affects the lives of people we never would have guessed. These are regular, good people who are hurting.

Another important truth about pornography viewing is that it occurs in degrees. In a 2015 *Ensign* article, President Dallin H. Oaks outlined the following four degrees:

1. Inadvertent Exposure: "A mistake [that] calls for correction rather than repentance."

2. Occasional Use: "May be occasional or even frequent, but it is always intentional, and that is its evil."
3. Intensive Use: "Repeated intentional use" that becomes almost involuntary.
4. Compulsive Use (Addiction): A dependency that "takes priority over almost everything else in life."[1]

While reading his words, it may or may not be obvious which category applies to your marriage. It wasn't obvious to me or my husband for a very long time.

Tumult of Opinions

One morning, I was awakened by the touch of Luke's clammy hand. He was nervous. I knew what this meant before I even opened my eyes. After ten years of being married to a "pornography addict," I had lived this cycle too many times to be taken by surprise.

I reluctantly opened my eyes, and his countenance confirmed it. With defeat in his voice and shame written on his face, he said, "I'm so sorry, Elizabeth. I relapsed last night."

We talked until he had to leave for work.

Before I went out to face my day of motherhood, I flipped onto my stomach, got on my knees, pulled the covers over my head, and began to pray. Pleas for understanding and direction stumbled out clumsily in between sobs.

The day before that relapse, Luke had a difficult interview for a bishopric calling with our well-meaning stake president. He seemed very frustrated with Luke's long pornography struggle and lost his temper during the interview. Ironically, that uncomfortable situation was what Luke had tried to cope with by viewing pornography the next day.

This was not too much of a surprise. Most of our leaders over the years have focused solely on sobriety. "When was the last time?" became their measuring stick of Luke, like a clock that would reset with

---

1. Dallin H. Oaks, "Recovering from the Trap of Pornography," *Ensign*, Oct. 2015, 36.

each relapse. How long of sobriety was long enough? No one really told him because no one really knew.

"Your wife is enabling you," the stake president said in exasperation. "She needs to get her head out of the sand and give you an ultimatum to make you stop!"

His words echoed in my mind as I knelt on my bed. "Please, Heavenly Father," I desperately begged. "Where do we go from here?"

I was so confused because for years Luke followed all of our leaders' suggestions, but still he would give in to temptation even though he didn't want to. He truly was improving though. His heart had become soft and repentant. He was having revelatory experiences with the Holy Ghost regularly. He was kind, patient, empathetic, and thoughtful. He was aware and helpful at home. He was even temple-worthy. The leaders who tried to help him through shame and fear could not deny the condition of his heart—his striving. He was dedicated to the Savior and never gave up.

These characteristics became even more solidified when he learned from a therapist that being mindful of his emotions was the key to success. The therapist taught him about escape and that being aware in the moment of temptation was the way to dethrone his addiction. He still had an addiction, he said, but sobriety wasn't the measuring stick of recovery—his heart was. And with time and consistent mindfulness, his sobriety would catch up with his heart.

"Is our stake president right, Heavenly Father?" I now demanded in my prayer. "Should we really try to reach sobriety with ultimatums? Or is the mindfulness path right and we just need to keep on it? We've been on it for so long now, and it feels as if something's missing. We've followed everyone's suggestions, but what are *Thy* suggestions?"

I continued: "I don't care what the answer is. I don't care if we've been right or wrong. I just want to know what Thou thinks! We know the Savior is the Deliverer, but which of these paths will help our marriage access the power of His Atonement to bring about that deliverance? We've been asking Thee this question for more than ten years. Luke has been asking for much, much longer. We know Thou hast never left us or him alone on our journey, but we're still so confused."

Never in my life had I felt so at one with the Prophet Joseph Smith. "In the midst of this . . . tumult of opinions, I often said to myself: What is to be done? Who of all these parties are right; or, are they all wrong together? If any one of them be right, which is it, and how shall I know it?" (Joseph Smith—History 1:10)

Interrupted by little tummies needing breakfast, I took a deep breath and closed my prayer. Moving forward with the hope that "someday, somehow, it will all work out" would have to suffice for now. *Again.*

✶✶✶✶✶✶

My prayer was answered, in fact, the very next day with this simple truth: Luke had been misdiagnosed, so to speak. His pornography struggle was an affliction, *not* an addiction.

This was an intensely important distinction. While we learned about many beneficial things over the years, the general treatment plan for Luke's sickness was based on addiction recovery and the twelve-step program. This medicine had healing properties, but because it was based on the wrong diagnosis, and therefore was the incorrect medicine, it never really had the potential to help Luke obtain complete healing.

I go into the details in this book about how we came to understand that Luke does not have an addiction. After we learned that, I started to wonder how many people had the same story as us. How many are out there confused, exhausted, and feeling defeated because they have been trying to recover from a "pornography addiction" that is *not* an addiction?

His Opportunity

I remember as a young single adult listening to President Jeffrey R. Holland talk about the lessons we can learn from the difficult time Joseph Smith endured while in Liberty Jail. "Every one of us," he said, "in one way or another, great or small, dramatic or incidental, is going to spend a little time in Liberty Jail— spiritually speaking."[2] I wondered then what my time in "Liberty Jail" would look like someday. What would happen in my life that would be incredibly hard yet so refining?

After now identifying at least one of my Liberty Jail life experiences as being in a marriage afflicted with pornography, I often go back and find comfort in the words I heard President Holland promise all those years ago:

> You can have sacred, revelatory, profoundly instructive experience with the Lord in the most miserable experiences of your life—in the worst settings, while enduring the most painful injustices, when facing the most insurmountable odds and opposition you have ever faced. . . .
>
> The lessons of the winter of 1838–39 teach us that every experience can become a redemptive experience if we remain bonded to our Father in Heaven through that difficulty. These difficult lessons teach us that *man's extremity is God's opportunity*, and if we will be humble and faithful, if we will be believing and not curse God for our problems, He can turn the unfair and inhumane and debilitating prisons of our lives into temples—or at least into a circumstance that can bring comfort and revelation, divine companionship and peace.[3]

I have since pondered on the truths that allowed our extremity to be God's opportunity—the truths that led us to have "sacred, revelatory, profoundly instructive experience[s] with the Lord" while still in our prison. This book is written to share those very things, particularly as they relate to me as the spouse.

To keep the focus on lessons learned rather than our specific journey, this book is not presented exactly chronologically. Instead, it is organized into three important categories of truths we discovered about *my life* as the spouse of someone struggling to stop viewing pornography:

---

2. Jeffrey R. Holland, "Lessons from Liberty Jail" (Brigham Young University devotional, Sept. 7, 2008), 4, speeches.byu.edu.

3. Jeffrey R. Holland, "Lessons from Liberty Jail," 4; emphasis added.

- **I Feel:** I have confusing, complex emotions that, when understood, can be worked through effectively.
- **I Need:** I have specific needs that, when addressed, will aid in my healing and that of my marriage. When I understand them, I will be able to ask for what I need from myself and from others.
- **I Can:** I can be enabled and strengthened by Jesus Christ to *act* in my circumstances instead of being *acted upon* by them.

Part 1: I Feel

I have confusing, complex emotions that when understood can be worked through effectively.

Some of the things I feel:

I feel like I'm going crazy.
I feel alone and want to hide.
I have trauma.
Underneath it all, I feel fear.

1
I feel like I'm going crazy

I couldn't form words when I first learned about Luke's relationship with pornography. We didn't consider at the time that it was an addiction, but we knew that whatever it was, it was harmful to us both. It was a darkness that consumed us.

I was about to leave for work when he told me he had been viewing pornography. He didn't tell me the full extent of it right then, but I felt like what he did tell me was all I could take.

I spent my whole nursing shift distracted by this huge weight now sitting on my chest. Small pieces of previous confusion started making sense. I had recently been feeling disconnected from Luke. He seemed emotionally unavailable and I didn't know why. I guess now I did.

Why It Hurts So Much

When a loved one has a habit of escape that causes disconnection, it affects their relationships with others. When viewing pornography is the habit, spouses are hurt in a unique way because it challenges almost every promise made at the altar. And when one is told that the habit is actually an addiction, and that times of viewing are relapses, hope is especially difficult to muster up. Any sense of control is trampled on, and powerlessness takes over.

After one of Luke's relapses in the early years of our marriage, I confided in my journal about the turmoil I was drowning in.

> This hurts on so many levels.
>
> It hurts me as his wife and eternal companion. Luke made a sacred covenant with me, and part of that is being morally chaste, faithful, and true to me. He's supposed to protect me from pain, not cause it. When he looks at pornography, I feel forgotten by him.
>
> It hurts me as his best friend. It's painful watching him hurt and struggle and be so angry with himself. I can tell he's hurting, and I feel powerless to stop it.
>
> It hurts me as his partner in intimacy. It's supposed to be just me and him exploring the world of sex together—not me without him or him without me or us with anyone else. If intimacy is engaged in outside the two of us, I feel like it degrades what we have. It makes our intimacy not as special, not as safe, not as secure, and not as needed. Part of my privilege as his wife is that I get to be the one to meet his needs in that way and vice versa. I don't want him to look elsewhere. It used to make me feel good that I was the only girl Luke had seen and known in that way; I was the only one who could make him feel those things, or so I thought. It's hard to feel like he really doesn't need me for any of that.
>
> It also hurts on a spiritual level. Watching him distance himself from the Lord is scary. What does this mean for our eternal life together? What does this do to the validity of our covenants? What does this mean for the spiritual protection in our home? It's also so heartbreaking because I want him to feel the peace and happiness of being close to the Lord. I want him to feel confident before Him always, and I can tell that He doesn't. What will this lead to? Will he leave the Church?

A Storm of Emotions

With time and frequent relapses, the initial numbness and shock turned into an array of emotions. I was angry. Sad. Optimistic. Hopeless. Hopeful. Self-conscious. Annoyed. Disappointed. Confused. Frustrated. Lonely. In denial. Anxious. Disgusted. Depressed. Over-sexual. Under-sexual. Rejected.

Because of the frequency of relapses, it felt like explosions kept going off before I could get my footing. It took a very long time for me to be able to organize, label, and process my feelings. I can put my experience into words now, but at the time, it felt like pure chaos.

Sometimes I would stay in an emotion for days or weeks. Other times I would go back and forth between emotions, one day feeling one and the next feeling another. Usually, though, I would feel a lot of things all at once or switch between them in a matter of minutes.

At times I wanted to know everything about Luke's behavior and choices. Other times I wanted to know nothing. I went through periods of trying to control every little part of his recovery efforts, and I went through periods of being completely apathetic to him and his recovery. I would also go between feeling hyper-sexual—which was very confusing to me—and having an intense distaste toward anything remotely related to sex.

I honestly felt like I was going crazy. The only pattern I ever noticed was that there was no pattern at all. I was completely at the mercy of whatever emotion overcame me at any given time. How long it would last and how intensely I would feel it was anyone's guess.

They Aren't Coming Out of Nowhere

The difficulty was that I couldn't put a name to any of my emotions, and neither could Luke.

I'm not sure who was more confused by my seemingly irrational behavior, me or him. I can remember getting overly annoyed that he didn't put the cereal box away one morning, not realizing that the root of my frustration was that he looked at pornography again. Or, when we later had kids, my anger with his choices would sometimes be displaced onto the kids through yelling at them for little things.

One reason it was hard to trace these feelings back to Luke's pornography viewing in the moment was because my thoughts and feelings surrounding a relapse could resurface long after it actually happened. Being annoyed about the cereal box could be weeks after he told me he relapsed. It all depended on how long the initial shock, denial, and numbness lasted before the array of emotions came on.

Most times we both would think we had moved on from the damage of a choice he had made, but in reality, I hadn't. The unhealed pain that was pushed down deep inside bubbled back up at the oddest times and in the strangest ways. What was happening to me? Was I going crazy? It really did seem like it.

2

I feel alone and want to hide

For the longest time throughout our marriage, I was on an emotional roller coaster. During every up, down, twist, and turn, one thing remained constant: I felt alone. Despite not wanting to feel this way, I hid from everyone, especially in the days and weeks following one of Luke's relapses.

I could feel the conflict within, and it made me feel even more like I was going crazy. No one consistently reached out to me with comfort and support, but how could they when barely anyone even knew? And if they did know about Luke's "addiction," they certainly didn't know how often he relapsed and what a huge part of our lives this problem was.

I thought no one would understand or even want to. Who could blame them? Everyone was having their own trials—why burden them with mine?

I knew that my Savior Jesus Christ understood. I tried to lean on Him daily. But the negativity and numbness that clouded most days masked His presence in my life. I clung to the moments when my pain was penetrated by the comforting presence of the Holy Ghost, allowing His light to break up the smoke and chaos of an explosion. Those moments kept me going, but they felt far less often than I needed.

I hated feeling so alone. A part of me, though, wanted to keep it that way. It's scary letting people in. There were times I did reach out but then quickly discovered the pain of sharing this part of my life with the wrong people. So I learned how to avoid the damaging sympathy from those who didn't know what to say: Just don't tell anyone.

Even if I wasn't socializing with the intention of sharing what I was going through, I still didn't want to be around anyone. It was overwhelming to pretend like everything was okay. Most days I didn't even have it in me to give my voice a cheerful tone.

So I stayed in. I didn't answer my phone. I barely responded to texts. I isolated myself and withdrew. It fed my loneliness but seemed a small price to pay to avoid the stress of socializing while having open, gaping wounds that people didn't know how to respond to.

3
I have trauma

IN THE EARLY YEARS, WE DID A LOT OF THINGS TO TRY TO FIX WHAT we thought was an addiction. We put filters and passwords on every device. We fasted and prayed for spiritual help. We did couples therapy and group therapy with sex addiction specialists who were also members of the Church. We sought out guidance from our bishop. We dove into books, online courses, and podcasts about pornography addiction, on our own and together. We felt we were doing all we could.

I can see now how all those resources were important bricks the Lord was able to strategically place and secure for us. He used them to create a path to the beautiful place we're at now. So I'm grateful for them. But at the time, I wasn't sure any of it was helping. The progress was slow. Most times it was so slow that it felt nonexistent.

IT TAKES A TOLL ON US BOTH

Despite all our efforts, I was still very much on that emotional roller coaster. I was numb from the shock of first learning about Luke's behavior. Then I spiraled into what seemed like irrational behaviors for years. Each relapse resulted in unpredictable emotions that kept me guessing day to day, hour to hour, and sometimes minute to minute what I would experience next. I had no idea what was going on inside; I didn't feel like *me* anymore.

Because we can only stay in a state of high stress for so long, after years of this coupled with wondering if our efforts were even helping, I became numb and in denial. My craziness subsided. I took each painful hit of relapse shrapnel silently with a somewhat forced smile.

I say *somewhat* because a huge part of me was actually happy. When Luke wasn't relapsing frequently, our marriage was filled with beauty, laughter, spirituality, and true connection. When he did relapse, I could tell he hated it just as much as I did, if not more. Shame was taking a toll on him. He was the one holding the grenade each time, and it was obvious that the explosions wounded him much more than they wounded me.

I was often filled with compassion for him. "It's okay. Everything will be okay," I would tell myself. "He's doing his best—I don't need to make him feel worse than he already feels." So I would try to ignore the fact that I was hurting too. And that was how we lived for a very long time.

Enlightenment and Understanding

One day, about five years into our marriage, I was driving down the road listening to an audiobook called *Strengthening Recovery Through Strengthening Marriage* by Dr. Kevin B. Skinner and Geoff Steurer.[4] In it they explained that attachment is "a primary survival need as important as food, water, shelter, and oxygen. . . . The need for us to reach out and connect and also to have somebody need us is essential to our survival as human beings." They went on to describe the two types of attachment we need.

The first type is an attachment that's supposed to be established parent-to-child. As the caregiver consistently responds to the child's needs, "the child gets the message over time that they're valuable,

---

4. Kevin B. Skinner and Geoff Steurer, "Strengthening Recovery Through Strengthening Marriage" (K. Skinner Corp., 2015), audio CD.

that they're loved, that they're safe; the world has order, it's predictable, they can count on knowing what they are going to get and what they're not going to get. It's a very safe, secure kind of system." This is a one-sided attachment relationship. The parent doesn't expect or need the child to respond to them in the same way for the bonding and connection to occur.

This first type of attachment gives rich meaning to our relationship with Deity and how Heavenly Father wants us to address Him. He is our Father. We are His children. He wants to teach us His pattern of this type of attachment.

The parent-child relationship is so important because it teaches us what healthy attachment and safety look like. It instills in us what it feels like to be valued. Then as we grow into adulthood, we look for a relationship where we can receive *and give* similar responsiveness, which brings us to the second type of attachment.

This type of attachment occurs adult-to-adult. Couples begin to form this early on and implement what they learned in their child-to-parent bond. They respond to and are there for each other through physical touch, service, being vulnerable, listening, and so forth.

This is not a one-sided form of attachment like the child-to-parent relationship. In order for a healthy attachment bond to form between a couple, both need to consistently reach out and turn to the other for connection. They need to be able to trust that their reaching out will be met with attentiveness by the other person.

As I listened to these two professionals teach me about attachment, I realized that I thought I had that type of attachment with Luke. But over time, I could feel distance grow between us, though I could never put my finger on why that left me feeling *so* abandoned. Just as I was thinking this to myself, they went on to explain:

> Where the danger of pornography, or the damage of it rather, happens to this relationship is that instead of turning to the relationship for comfort, security, reassurance, and safety, he's reaching for something else. This is exactly where it hits the heart of the relationship, that turning away. That's where the damage is . . . there's now a second attachment competing for that primary relationship.

When she feels that disconnection, because her need for closeness is a survival need, . . . it will oftentimes, well, in every case that I've seen for that matter, throw her into a set of reactive behaviors as a way to try and cope with the disconnection and the trauma of losing the safety of that attachment. She has to get [attachment] somewhere. And if she can't find it, then you're going to see an increase in stress levels, an increase perhaps in anger, or in solemness, or in sad depression because she feels hopeless or like "I can never compete with those images." . . . She needs a safe place where she can be open about her hurts, her pains, her fears. This is why women literally feel like they are going crazy. . . .

You know, you take off somebody's oxygen when they are climbing a high mountain, and they start to become disoriented and panicked; that's exactly what happens when she discovers that he's not there anymore or that this whole time he's not been available and he's been bonding with this other thing.

The reality is that these are women who are . . . dealing with a crazy-making situation of "How do I get attached to somebody who's not available to me?"

The other thing that pornography does is it makes men more cut off from their own emotions and their own sensitivity and feelings. And so you have this double shot of "He's turning away from me but he's also turning away from himself." He's almost twice as unavailable than he would normally be if he was connected and attached.

No, she's not going crazy—[the] oxygen has been pulled out and she's sucking wind trying to get air from somewhere. And he's over here probably feeling his own guilt, not knowing how to give her that oxygen because he's the one who . . . pulled [it].[5]

What I learned that day about myself was a pivotal point in my journey of healing. Even though on the surface I looked like I was doing fine, inside I had wounds that I wanted to understand, and probably more desperately, I wanted someone else to understand as well. Driving in my car with mascara-stained tears streaming down my face, I finally felt like the chaos I had been trying to make sense of

---

5. Skinner and Steurer, "Strengthening Recovery Through Strengthening Marriage."

for so long wasn't chaotic after all. That validation and clarity helped me start to wade through my emotional confusion and the situation my marriage was in.

For years I had been gasping for breath and panicking as I struggled to find my footing in a secure, stable, oxygen-filled place. I could clearly see now *what* I was feeling and *why* it felt so traumatic. This was the explanation behind what my therapist called "betrayal trauma," a trauma that spouses of those who repeatedly view pornography often suffer from.

What a relief to finally understand. I wasn't going crazy! I was feeling the absence of a basic survival need—attachment—and was having a trauma response as a result. Maybe now I could explain it to Luke because I'm sure he thought I was going crazy too.

4
Underneath it all, I feel fear

"You had a trigger, Elizabeth."

"Trigger?" I didn't understand what my therapist was talking about. I thought Luke, as the one addicted, was the one who had triggers—those seemingly small things that would happen to or around him that would make him have an urge to "act out," to masturbate or look at pornography.

"Trigger of what?" I asked.

"As the one betrayed, you have your own triggers. They're things that trigger your trauma, your fear."

My face must have still looked confused because he went on to explain: "Have you ever laid in bed trying to go to sleep when all of a sudden, you hear a noise? Fear surges through your body and your mind begins to fill in the blanks. 'What was that?' you wonder. Before you know it, your fear has convinced you there's an intruder in the house who's about to open your bedroom door and murder you."

Yep. He pegged me. I'm definitely a "check all the locks in the house three times before I go to bed" type of girl.

He continued, "What happens next in that scenario? You have a physical reaction to the things your mind is telling you. You get all sweaty and nervous. You lie there paralyzed, afraid of what your mind has told you the rest of the night will look like. It's the same thing with betrayal trauma."

He told me things could happen that may seem small or insignificant to other people, but because of what I've experienced within my marriage, those things might heavily affect me. They could trigger my fear and send me into a series of reactive behaviors, thoughts, and feelings.

Maybe a scene in a movie where the man is unfaithful triggers me, and I constantly ask Luke in the days that follow how he's doing in his recovery. Or maybe Luke and I are walking in the store together and we pass by a very immodest woman. I may feel triggered to assume he was triggered by her and now wants to act out in lust. That might lead me to emotionally withdraw and be quiet and closed off the rest of the day, perhaps without even realizing why.

Not Always Obvious

One of the most common triggers for me turned out to be very difficult to identify. I finally made the connection early one morning after I came home from work. I was a labor and delivery nurse at the time and would often work well into the early morning hours. After one particularly long and draining shift, I came home at 4 a.m. to a completely spotless apartment. It was a surprise considering we had a very rambunctious toddler at the time.

The anxiety that cleanliness threw me into was more than my overly tired heart and mind could handle. I immediately went into our bedroom, sat down on the bed, and gently shook Luke awake.

"Luke . . . Luke . . . Did you relapse while I was at work?"

"What?" His sleepy response intensified my panic and I started sobbing.

"Luke! Did you relapse? Please just tell me, did you relapse?!"

I couldn't catch my breath now, and my gasping instinctively made him sit up and hold my shoulders to see if I was okay. Awake now and hearing pieces of my desperate question in between my sobs, he understood what was happening.

"No. No, Elizabeth, I didn't relapse." Tenderly grabbing my face, he stared into my puffy eyes. "Look at me—I didn't relapse. It's okay."

My crying slowed down as I buried my wet face into his chest. Holding me, he whispered into my ear, "Why did you think I relapsed?"

I slowly pulled out of the hug as I realized for the first time what the trigger was.

"Every time you relapse, you start cleaning or doing the dishes or vacuuming. Every time. As soon as you can after a relapse, you clean. Well, tonight you cleaned the whole apartment. It's spotless! I was afraid you relapsed again."

Without realizing it himself, Luke had gotten into the habit of trying to do whatever he could to minimize the blow of another relapse on me. Of course, after a relapse wasn't the only time he cleaned or helped out around the house. But cleaning was something he would do to try to decrease the stress and pain that he knew a disclosure would cause me when he did view pornography, and I guess my aching, traumatized heart picked up on it. I subconsciously labeled his thoughtful efforts as a sign of potential pain, almost as if to say "Caution: Danger up ahead!"

Underneath the Triggered Reactions

Whether a trigger was obvious or not, it could have a variety of possible effects on me. But underneath them all—underneath the nagging, the assumptions, the withdrawal, and the panic attacks—is fear. Fear of the unknown. Fear of abandonment. Fear of another explosion and having my oxygen taken away once again.

One morning, Luke's phone went off and woke me up. I saw the notification as I went to silence it. It was a video chat invite from a girl with a sexy profile picture. Within the previous two-week period, Luke had finished graduate school, we moved to another state, and we had our third child. We were living with his parents over the

Christmas holiday while waiting to close on our new house. It was a time of many stressors, all of which seemed to take priority over any efforts related to Luke's addiction (or what we thought was an addiction at the time). I was in a major phase of exhaustion and denial.

When I saw that notification though, emotions started boiling up inside of me that I hadn't felt so intensely in a very long time: anger, sadness, abandonment, loneliness, pain, betrayal.

Why, though? I knew he didn't video-chat with her—it was just spam. He couldn't have controlled that invite coming in any more than any of us can control what's sent to our email's junk folder.

But what if I didn't get this notification first? Would he have clicked on the video chat? "No, he wouldn't have," I thought to myself. "He wouldn't cheat on me with a *real* person." And then it hit me like a ton of bricks: The people doing pornography *are* real people.

In that moment, I felt like infidelity was rampant in our marriage, and it brought me out of my state of denial. I started panicking right there, holding Luke's phone while lying in bed next to him sleeping. I couldn't breathe but also somehow couldn't stop crying. (The paradox of panic, I guess.)

When Luke woke up, I didn't want him to touch me or even look at me. It felt like I was going through every emotion I could possibly feel, but at the same time, I felt numb. Yet another paradox. I thought I would spontaneously combust.

It took weeks and an online course by our therapist to rebuild our connection with each other and with the Lord. The level of vulnerability, hard work, and humility that was required of us led us to feel bonded and close. I felt heard—*really* heard.

In fact, I felt so heard that I truly thought he wouldn't hurt me or our relationship ever again with pornography. I was the priority now and so was our marriage. With that, we settled into our new house, life, and what felt like a new marriage.

A few months later, I drove with the kids to my in-laws for a doctor's appointment. Luke had to work so he stayed behind. After driving five hours with a newborn and two toddlers on my own, I pulled into the driveway at midnight. I tried transferring my sleeping kids seamlessly into the house but failed miserably. It wasn't until 2 a.m. that I finally was able to go to bed myself. It was a long day to say the least.

Exhausted, I lay on the bed and grabbed my phone to charge it. When I did, I noticed a missed call and a voicemail from Luke.

He had relapsed.

I could feel myself start to shut down as the voicemail played. Then I curled into a ball on the bed, shut my eyes, and went into my familiar numb place.

One night after we returned home, we were eating dinner as a family. All of a sudden, the pain and anger I had been suppressing the whole trip took control of me. I verbally exploded on Luke about him relapsing while we were gone. I even threw a plastic spoon at him that I was using to feed one of the kids. Then I collapsed on the ground in tears.

Our oldest toddler came running over, wrapped her arms around me, and yelled, "Daddy, stop it! Stop making Mama sad!" She didn't know what he did, but I felt so awful that I put her and the others through that moment of confusion, fear, and instability.

Lying there crying, I realized I couldn't take it anymore. Had the last several months since that video-chat trigger meant nothing? When we talked about the relapse while I was still on the trip, I went back to my old ways, suppressing my feelings, not wanting to hurt Luke, and being too emotionally drained to do anything else except lean into the sentiment of "It's okay, you'll get 'em next time." But as I laid on that kitchen floor, I honestly wasn't sure he would "get 'em next time."

Wanting to prevent another outburst, I tried my best to process my feelings that night in my journal:

> I'm so much more closed off now than I was after the video chat invite thing because I feel like my trust and hope in his desire to change is fading. Does he even want to stop? I guess I'm not so sure anymore, which is making me withdraw. I'm not going to walk into the same painful trap I've been walking into for years and years. Nothing about his efforts seems to change, not for long anyway—otherwise, he'd be done with pornography for good! So then why do I expect or think or hope that his behavior will change? No, I'll

protect myself now from being so hurt the next time he relapses. I mean, that's why I'm hurting this bad now—because I was so vulnerable and so open and trusting and hopeful. I really thought that was it—that we had reached the end of relapses. How stupid can I be?

Looking back, I really could have just written, "I'm afraid."

Part 2:
I Need

I have specific needs that, when addressed, will aid in my healing and that of my marriage. When I understand them, I will be able to ask for what I need from myself and from others.

Some of the things I need:

I need to learn.
I need the Book of Mormon.
I need to believe.
I need trust to be rebuilt.
I need to be careful too.
I need to heal.
I need support and connection.

5
I need to learn

IN THE EARLY PART OF OUR MARRIAGE, I THOUGHT OUR FAITH IN God would, on its own, simply rid our marriage of the parasite that pornography had become. However, I quickly learned that the Lord wanted us to show "[our] faith by [our] works" because "faith, if it hath not works, is dead, being alone" (James 2:17–18).

So Luke and I started seeing a therapist together who was also a faithful member of the Church. We wanted our therapist to understand our beliefs and covenants. After some time, we began attending separate therapy groups for husbands and wives run by our therapist where we could learn specifically about sex addiction.

It was incredibly eye-opening. We came to understand all sorts of things, like the parts of the brain that deal with decision-making. We also gained many new tools to better handle emotions, communicate effectively, and not be such a slave to our thoughts. After years, though, we began to feel like we were spinning our wheels. Luke was still relapsing very frequently, and both of our hearts were still broken.

We talked about it with a dear friend and mentor who could relate to Luke's types of wounds from personal experience. He wisely counseled us to incorporate the Savior more into our efforts. Without realizing it, we had put all our focus on the neurological aspects of addiction and the psychological techniques we had learned in therapy to help us heal.

His gentle invitation reminded me of a similar invitation the Savior gave us all in Doctrine and Covenants 88:118: "Seek learning, even by study *and also* by faith" (emphasis added).

Once Luke was proactive in using the skills he learned in therapy while simultaneously "feasting upon the word of Christ" (2 Nephi 31:20), he began to experience consistent change for the first time. And when I found the same balance, my heart started to actually mend. It took years to get to that point and required humility, patience, and hard work. But we had finally gained some traction and could see a visible path to lasting peace. Even though relapses still occurred fairly often, our learning allowed us to start being "empowered through the Atonement to *act* as agents (see Doctrine and Covenants 58:26–29) and *impact* [our] circumstances."[6] Even if it was only little by little.

---

6. David A. Bednar, "Bear Up Their Burdens with Ease," *Ensign* or *Liahona*, May 2014, 89.

6
I need the Book of Mormon

"No one is doing it, Mom! Youth conference is almost here, and no one will have read the Book of Mormon by then. Why did I even make this challenge?"

My seventeen-year-old sister, Mae, sounded heartbroken. I stood in the hallway with my head leaning against our bedroom doorframe so I could listen unnoticed. Her voice cracked and she began to cry.

"I don't just want them to read it because of the challenge—I also want them to feel the spirit of it! They're missing out on so much and will get way more out of youth conference if they come having had their own experiences with the Book of Mormon. That's the whole point! That's why Sister Christensen and I came up with the challenge, but no one is doing it!"

Her words pierced my fourteen-year-old heart. *I* was one of the youth not doing it. I decided then and there that I couldn't let her down. That night, I opened up the Book of Mormon with the intention of reading the whole thing for the first time. I knew I probably wouldn't be able to finish it before youth conference a few weeks later, but I wanted to read as much as I possibly could before then.

It was summertime, so I had a lot of opportunities to read. At first, I did it just because I didn't want Mae to feel bad, but at some point along the way, my motivation changed. I couldn't put it down—I didn't want to. I read constantly. I stayed up late and got up early. Day after day, I was filled with a joy I hadn't experienced before with such consistency.

One afternoon, I sat alone on the floor of Mae's and my bedroom, reading between our queen bed and the wall. My back was against the bed frame, and I had my feet kicked up to rest on the wall. Above my feet was a large window that let the warm Arizona sun shine down on me. In my cozy seclusion, I opened up the Book of Mormon and began where I had left off before lunch. It was the account of Nephi and Lehi in Helaman 5 when they were wrongfully imprisoned by the Lamanites for preaching the gospel of Jesus Christ.

The events that took place in the prison captivated me. They were starving and had been mistreated for many days when, suddenly, a protecting pillar of fire surrounded them. Darkness fell over everyone else in the prison, especially over the Lamanites who were holding them captive. The prison walls began to tremble, and the voice of the Lord called their oppressors to repentance multiple times. Picturing the scene vividly in my mind, I continued reading:

> 34 And it came to pass that the Lamanites could not flee because of the cloud of darkness which did overshadow them; yea, and also they were immovable because of the fear which did come upon them.
>
> 35 Now there was one among them who was a Nephite by birth, who had once belonged to the church of God but had dissented from them.
>
> 36 And it came to pass that he turned him about, and behold, he saw through the cloud of darkness the faces of Nephi and Lehi; and behold, they did shine exceedingly, even as the faces of angels. And he beheld that they did lift their eyes to heaven; and they were

in the attitude as if talking or lifting their voices to some being whom they beheld.

37 And it came to pass that this man did cry unto the multitude, that they might turn and look. And behold, there was power given unto them that they did turn and look; and they did behold the faces of Nephi and Lehi.

38 And they said unto the man: Behold, what do all these things mean, and who is it with whom these men do converse?

39 Now the man's name was Aminadab. And Aminadab said unto them: They do converse with the angels of God.

40 And it came to pass that the Lamanites said unto him: What shall we do, that this cloud of darkness may be removed from overshadowing us?

41 And Aminadab said unto them: You must repent, and cry unto the voice, even until ye shall have faith in Christ, who was taught unto you by Alma, and Amulek, and Zeezrom; and when ye shall do this, the cloud of darkness shall be removed from overshadowing you.

42 And it came to pass that they all did begin to cry unto the voice of him who had shaken the earth; yea, they did cry even until the cloud of darkness was dispersed.

43 And it came to pass that when they cast their eyes about, and saw that the cloud of darkness was dispersed from overshadowing them, behold, they saw that they were encircled about, yea every soul, by a pillar of fire.

44 And Nephi and Lehi were in the midst of them; yea, they were encircled about; yea, they were as if in the midst of a flaming fire, yet it did harm them not, neither did it take hold upon the walls of the prison; and they were filled with that joy which is unspeakable and full of glory.

45 And behold, the Holy Spirit of God did come down from heaven, and did enter into their hearts, and they were filled as if with fire, and they could speak forth marvelous words.

46 And it came to pass that there came a voice unto them, yea, a pleasant voice, as if it were a whisper, saying:

47 Peace, peace be unto you, because of your faith in my Well Beloved, who was from the foundation of the world.

48 And now, when they heard this they cast up their eyes as if to behold from whence the voice came; and behold, they saw the

heavens open; and angels came down out of heaven and ministered unto them.

49 And there were about three hundred souls who saw and heard these things; and they were bidden to go forth and marvel not, neither should they doubt.

As I read, a brightness and warmth started moving within me, like a slow, peaceful sunrise. Once it consumed every part of me, it spilled out and filled the room! I felt like I was among the three hundred souls who were encircled about with a pillar of fire in the prison that day, learning for themselves for the first time what it means to have the heavens open for them. Then, all at once, the heavens opened for me and I knew this book was true. I knew it for myself. No one could have given me that powerful knowledge or that divinely intricate experience except God.

I don't even know if I ever told Mae that I overheard her conversation and that it was the catalyst for my own personal conversion. But it was, and it started for me a beautiful relationship with the Savior through the Book of Mormon. That incredible book became my companion during my awkward teenage years. It was my Liahona during my young single adult years. And throughout my marriage, it has become my balm of Gilead, a beautifully reliable source of comfort.

Why That Story?

Several years into marriage, I was reading the Book of Mormon one morning when my mind went back, as it had many times before, to that life-changing afternoon so many years ago. But this morning was different. For the first time, I wondered why that story. Why did the Lord wait 379 pages to give me my Moroni 10:4–5 answer? Or why did He not wait until I actually got to Moroni 10:4–5? I pondered on it all day.

That afternoon, I took my young kids swimming. As I sat watching them splash in the baby pool, it dawned on me. In that prison, Nephi and Lehi had a "sacred, revelatory, profoundly instructive experience with the Lord in [one of] the most miserable experiences of [their] life—in [one of] the worst settings, while enduring the most painful injustices, [and] when facing the most insurmountable odds and opposition."[7] The heavens opened for Nephi and Lehi despite the harsh conditions they were in due to no fault of their own. They had their own Liberty Jail experience! And so did the Lamanites who committed the injustices against them and against God!

I had already realized years earlier that being in a marriage afflicted by pornography was my own Liberty Jail experience—or rather, an experience where the Lord is able to "turn the unfair and inhumane and debilitating prisons of our lives into temples—or at least into a circumstance that can bring comfort and revelation, divine companionship and peace."[8] This rich symbolism and remarkable timing told me that God not only knows me and that He will continue to turn *my* trial into a temple, like he did for Nephi and Lehi, but that He will also do that for Luke like he did for the Lamanites who were also in the prison.

In His omniscience, my Heavenly Father knew way back when I was fourteen years old that I would one day need this specific hope and this divine message. And I would need—*desperately* need—the book that brought it to me.

Cling or Convert

I was studying Lehi's dream one night before bed. It was the first time I tried using a study guide while reading the Book of Mormon. I had just read about a group of people who started on the path toward the tree of life but "did lose their way, that they wandered off and were lost" (1 Nephi 8:23). Certain the righteous group would be next, I continued with the next verse: "And it came to pass that I beheld others pressing forward . . ." (verse 24).

"Pressing forward. Oh, yes," I thought to myself, "this has got to be the group I'm in."

". . . and caught hold of the end of the rod of iron; and they did press forward through the mist of darkness, clinging to the rod of iron, even until they did come forth and partake of the fruit of the tree."

---

7. Jeffrey R. Holland, "Lessons from Liberty Jail" (Brigham Young University devotional, Sept. 7, 2008), 3–4, speeches.byu.edu.
8. Jeffrey R. Holland, "Lessons from Liberty Jail," 4.

Inspired by the imagery, I was even more sure now. "Okay, yes! This is definitely who I want to be. 'Clinging!'—they held on so tight to that iron rod, and that's why they made it to the tree! I want to be just like that!"

Pleased with what I thought I had just learned, I read on: "And after they had tasted of the fruit they were ashamed, because of those that were scoffing at them; and they fell away into forbidden paths and were lost" (1 Nephi 8:28).

Utter shock. These were the ones who pressed forward and *clung* to the iron rod! How could they have fallen away? I felt so discouraged, as if nothing could overpower the influence of the adversary if his scoffing even got to the clingers. Would I eventually fall away too?

Thankfully I turned to my study guide and read this quote from Elder David A. Bednar: "Clinging to the rod of iron suggests to me only occasional 'bursts' of study or irregular dipping rather than consistent, ongoing immersion in the word of God."[9] It made so much sense! If you're clinging to an iron rod, you wouldn't be able to cling for very long before you'd have to let go to give your hands a break. There is no way you'd physically be able to cling the entire way.

Now compare that to another group Nephi saw: "And they came and caught hold of the end of the rod of iron; and they did press their way forward, *continually holding fast* to the rod of iron, until they came forth and fell down and partook of the fruit of the tree" (1 Nephi 8:30; emphasis added). Continually holding fast—meaning they were consistently holding on to the iron rod, and the brief moments they let go (because they're not perfect) were just that: brief. They held fast, quickly grabbing hold again and getting back on track. This beautiful, encouraging truth sank deep into my heart. I wasn't going to be a clinger, and I didn't need to be perfect. I was going to continually hold *fast*.

Many years and countless explosions later . . . I wrote the following in my journal:

---

9. John S. Bushman, Reed Romney, John R. Manis, and Curt R. Wakefield, *Teaching the Book of Mormon: Part 1 (1 Nephi–Alma 16)* (Cedar Fort, 2013), 27.

I learned something by the Spirit tonight—something really important about myself. When I'm suffering, I shut down and try to wait the suffering out. Almost like I hibernate. I hunker down and try to wait out the storm. This is not a good thing. It reminds me of the people in Lehi's dream who cling to the iron rod. I remember once I was studying that verse years ago feeling like "That's what I do! I cling to the rod! Good job, me!" only to find out that the next verses say those people partake of the fruit and then fall away. I remember realizing that for the first time and being so confused. "But they clung!" I thought clinging was the goal.

But then I read a quote by Elder Bednar. He taught that the word *cling* portrays the idea that they weren't secure or consistent enough in their conversion, symbolizing people who live life in spurts of spiritual effort followed by long breaks from it. Instead, it's better to immerse ourselves with the Spirit each day because this consistency builds lasting conversion and changes one's nature. The bursts or irregular dipping, as he put it, followed by long breaks are like moments of clinging. They lead to surface-level conversion because it's surface-level effort. Then, when hardship comes, when mocking comes, when questions come, when suffering comes, this type of conversion is not deep enough to withstand the trying winds.

This is what I realized I do. This is how I cope with stress. I don't lean *into* my faith; I don't just keep going in my consistent efforts. I shut down.

Actually, when I'm holding on to the iron rod and walking along, I don't think I'm clinging—I think I'm very much consistent with my efforts. But then a mist of darkness comes, like Luke relapsing, and I become insanely depressed and sit down on the path. That's what it feels like. I just want to sit and close my eyes and wait for the mist of darkness to pass, and then I can get back up and resume everything. But it's *in the mist of darkness* that I need the Spirit and God's word the most! Wow, I really am not long-suffering at all, am I?! Haha. I guess it's not really funny. I think I'm just embarrassed to have learned this hard truth about myself.

And the worst part is, the reason I realized this is because I'm doing it right now and have been sitting down for over a year. I stopped feeding spirits consistently [what we call our morning devotional with the kids over breakfast]. I stopped connecting with the Lord consistently. I stopped reading the Book of Mormon consistently. I stopped getting regular, reliable sleep, which I know messes with my hormones and makes everything worse. Emotionally and spiritually, I'm just sitting down, waiting for this mist to be done, telling myself that when it's all over, *then* I will stand back up and keep pressing forward. But that's so unrealistic. If I wait until my trials end, I'll be waiting forever.

I don't want to react this way to suffering. I don't want to sit down. I want to press on, continually holding fast. This is a weakness of mine that I've been blessed to have been pointed out to me by the Spirit. The Savior promised us that if we brought our weaknesses to Him, He would make them strengths. How though? What specifically do I need to do to stand back up even though this mist isn't over yet? And better still, stay standing up and stay moving forward? Well, like anything else the Lord is involved in, I need to do it line upon line. I'll just take one small step. Then another. Then another. And continue on like that. I don't need to make a huge grandiose spiritual effort to turbo-boost myself back up because the unnatural force of such an effort will cause me to lose my footing and come crashing back to the ground.

Now that I've realized this, I'm lying here trying to think what the first line (upon line) should be. But you know what? I think praying and asking God would be more productive than just asking myself!

Want to know what God told me that first line was? Read the Book of Mormon. Read it every day. Of all of the things I was "sitting down" on, that was what He wanted me to start with. And I found out why.

The key to continually holding fast is to do so *because you love the Lord and feel His love for you*. Not because you know you're supposed to. Not because it's on your to-do list or because you're trying to do everything perfectly. Not for the praise of others, or for any other reason except that you're converted, "which means being filled with our Savior's love."[10] Consistently being filled with God's love is the way to avoid clinging and sitting because when we are filled with such love, we naturally have a desire to live like Him and with Him, in this life and the next.

---

10. Robert D. Hales, "'Come, Follow Me' by Practicing Christian Love and Service," *Ensign* or *Liahona*, Nov. 2016, 23.

God's Opportunity

Because of how potently God's love can enter our hearts each time we partake of it, "the Book of Mormon, . . . [when] combined with the Spirit of the Lord, is the most powerful tool of conversion."[11] It's so powerful that even my four-year-old daughter could feel it:

> Last night, I lay with Annie and read to her from the Book of Mormon. I read Moroni 10 to her. She memorized verse 5 about four months ago, and I wanted to read that chapter so she could pick out that verse. It was sweet to see her face light up when she heard it as I read. We were able to discuss the context of the verse and she seemed to really love that.
>
> Then I kept reading. I was so pulled in by Moroni's words that I read the whole chapter out loud, even after she fell asleep. It had been such a long time since I'd read it in its entirety.
>
> It was truly a much-needed experience. I've been having so much self-doubt lately and my anxiety has been really bad—worse than it has been in a long time. While I read, though, the Spirit entered my heavy heart and filled it with God's love for me and for my efforts in the many trials of my life and marriage.
>
> I am so grateful for the Book of Mormon and the power of God that I can access, learn of, and feel by reading and living the principles inside it. It always amazes me that I can obtain peace from it without fail. It's like the Book of Mormon is so true, so good, so pure, and so untouched by Satan that one cannot help but be distanced from him and brought closer to God through it. I need that—I really do. God is the only one who can help me see clearly in my anxious state. When I feel that anxiety, it can become impossible to function, difficult to even breathe and think and . . . be. But He somehow guides me through it all. He brings me out of the darkness in my life and strengthens me to not give up or give way to the hopelessness that anxiety worships.
>
> The other thing I thought about as I read is that the Book of Mormon is *the* tool of conversion. It really simplifies our efforts to not be the elect who are deceived and misled. There are so many good things we can do, but reading the Book of Mormon is *the* thing to always make sure we are doing because it is *the* tool that will keep us filled with God's love. It was written for that purpose—to

---

11. Shayne M. Bowen, "The Role of the Book of Mormon in Conversion," *Ensign* or *Liahona*, Nov. 2018, 83.

> help us hold on to the iron rod instead of wandering on strange roads unprotected where we are out in the open, vulnerable to Satan's merciless war tactics. I think too many times, people forget we're in a war. I guess that's one good thing about being married to someone who struggles with pornography—I can't forget.

Out of all the resources we have used against the darkness that has fallen upon our marriage, nothing compares in significance to the Book of Mormon: Another Testament of Jesus Christ. That's because the One it is a testament of is the only One with the power to disperse that darkness.

> It is not just that the Book of Mormon teaches us truth, though it indeed does that. It is not just that the Book of Mormon bears testimony of Christ, though it indeed does that, too. But there is something more. There is a power in the book which will begin to flow into your lives the moment you begin a serious study of the book. You will find greater power to resist temptation. You will find the power to avoid deception. You will find the power to stay on the strait and narrow path. The scriptures are called "the words of life" (Doctrine and Covenants 84:85), and nowhere is that more true than it is of the Book of Mormon. When you begin to hunger and thirst after those words, you will find life in greater and greater abundance.[12]

I've learned by experience that I can keep my heart soft by storing beauty and truth inside of it, and you can too. So read the Book of Mormon. Read it every day. Allow it to be your companion, your Liahona, your balm of Gilead. Allow Heavenly Father to reveal the hidden messages of hope meant just for you that I know He has embedded in its pages.

If you let Him, He will use the Book of Mormon to surround you with a pillar of fire, open the heavens, and instill in you His sure love. So "go forth and marvel not, neither should [you] doubt" (Helaman 5:49) even during your darkest moments when you feel like all you can do is sit down.

---

12. *Teachings of Presidents of the Church: Ezra Taft Benson* (2014), 141.

7
I need to believe

Addiction. My understanding of this word has changed a lot over the years. I used to think it was only an issue for other people. Until it wasn't. I used to think it only applied to things like drugs and alcohol. Until it didn't.

But was Luke's unwanted habit an addiction? A true, full-fledged, would-die-without-it addiction? That is what all the experts told us. This had gone on for so long—how could it not be? When I read President Oaks' *Ensign* article[13] outlining the different levels of pornography viewing (see the introduction of this book), the conditioning I had for years led me to instantly, almost automatically, identify our situation as being in the addiction category.

Whatever was truly the level of Luke's pornography viewing, one thing always felt certain: Pornography seemed impossible for him to get out from under. The difficulty of overcoming pornography is illustrated in a letter written to President Oaks several years ago. In it,

---

13. Dallin H. Oaks, "Recovering from the Trap of Pornography," *Ensign*, Oct. 2015, 36.

the man who wrote the letter said, "In my eyes cocaine doesn't hold a candle to this. I have done both. . . . Quitting even the hardest drugs was nothing compared to [trying to quit pornography]."[14]

There was a time I believed pornography was stronger than Luke, stronger than us, stronger than our covenants—that is, until the Lord taught me it wasn't.

If Thou Wouldst Believe

Even in our pain, we can come to wholeheartedly believe that our spouses are capable of complete and lasting change—that they can be made whole, that they can be agents who act in righteousness instead of being acted upon by a faulty need for escape or a powerful urge to lust. President Boyd K. Packer taught that because of the Atonement of Jesus Christ, "save for those few who defect to perdition after having known a fulness, there is no habit, no addiction, no rebellion, no transgression, no offense exempted from the promise of complete forgiveness. . . . This knowledge should be as comforting to the innocent as it is to the guilty."[15] No matter which of these labels applies to our husbands, the Savior perfectly understands how to heal the damage caused by their sexual, sinful escapes. And the best part is that He wants to. As Elder Dale G. Renlund taught:

> Since God uses disease as a metaphor for sin throughout the scriptures, it is reasonable to ask, "How does Jesus Christ react when faced with our metaphorical diseases—our sins?" After all, the Savior said that He "cannot look upon sin with the least degree of allowance"; so how can He look at us, imperfect as we are, without recoiling in horror and disgust?
>
> The answer is simple and clear. As the Good Shepherd, Jesus Christ views disease in His sheep as a condition that needs treatment, care, and compassion. This shepherd, our Good Shepherd, finds joy in seeing His diseased sheep progress toward healing.[16]

---

14. Dallin H. Oaks, "Pornography," *Ensign* or *Liahona*, May 2005, 89.
15. Boyd K. Packer, "The Brilliant Morning of Forgiveness," *Ensign*, Nov. 1995, 19–20.
16. Dale G. Renlund, "Our Good Shepherd," *Ensign* or *Liahona*, May 2017, 30.

Once, while I was reading the New Testament at a time of hopelessness, the Spirit opened my eyes to see the story of Lazarus in a way I never had before.

It began as it always had. Jesus Christ received word that a friend of His was sick—so sick that this illness sent the man's loved ones into a state of worry and panic (see John 11:1–3).

"I know that feeling. Luke is sick because of pornography," I thought to myself as I read.

"When Jesus heard that, he said, This sickness is not unto death, but for the glory of God, that the Son of God might be glorified thereby" (John 11:4).

Jesus loved Lazarus and his family (see John 11:5). He knew how serious Lazarus's sickness had been. He even knew of his death (John 11:4, 11–14). Yet He still waited until Lazarus was dead for four whole days before going to minister to him and his sisters (see John 11:6–7).

As I continued, a picture formed in my mind. Luke's relationship with pornography was killing him. It was killing him spiritually as his repetitive sins turned him further away from God. It was also killing him physically. It was literally changing his brain, altering his desires, thoughts, and behaviors. Were he to continue on that path, he would become unrecognizable, and the man I married would no longer exist.

The slow, painful death that pornography was causing in Luke was placing him in a dark tomb of isolation. It laid him there, wrapped in tight, binding graveclothes that kept him unable to move or get out by himself. He was powerless. I was powerless. And the longer his disease went untreated, the more I wondered at what point he would be too dead for anyone, even the Savior, to intervene effectively. "Could Christ not have just prevented this all?" With these concerns in my heart, I continued reading:

> 37 And some of them said, Could not this man, which opened the eyes of the blind, have caused that even this man should not have died?
>
> 38 Jesus therefore again groaning in himself cometh to the grave. It was a cave, and a stone lay upon it.

39 Jesus said, Take ye away the stone. Martha, the sister of him that was dead, saith unto him, Lord, by this time he stinketh: for he hath been dead four days.

40 Jesus saith unto her, Said I not unto thee, that, if thou wouldest believe, thou shouldest see the glory of God?

41 Then they took away the stone from the place where the dead was laid. And Jesus lifted up his eyes, and said, Father, I thank thee that thou hast heard me.

42 And I knew that thou hearest me always: but because of the people which stand by I said it, that they may believe that thou hast sent me.

43 And when he thus had spoken, he cried with a loud voice, Lazarus, come forth.

44 And he that was dead came forth, bound hand and foot with graveclothes: and his face was bound about with a napkin. Jesus saith unto them, Loose him, and let him go.

45 Then many of the Jews which came to Mary, and had seen the things which Jesus did, believed on him. (John 11:37–45)

Jesus Christ's intention was never to prevent Lazarus's disease or the pain and death that accompanied it. Nor was His intention to prevent the heartache that it brought to his friends and sisters. He consciously allowed the events of mortality and agency to unfold in their lives.

His goal was to show them that because of His atoning sacrifice, He could take that pain, that death, that heartache and make it purposeful—and then, as if that weren't enough, breathe life back into all those who experienced it. By so doing, every witness to this miracle would "see the glory of God" (John 11:40) and "believe on him" (John 11:45).

With tears in my eyes, I put my New Testament down. Pondering the Spirit's message to me, I wondered how long our "four days" would be. When would the Savior raise Luke from the dead? And would our marriage be able to rise with him?

Hope filled me as I glanced down and found verse 40 again: "Said I not unto thee, that, if thou wouldest believe, thou shouldest see the glory of God?"

8
I need trust to be rebuilt

"Did you have a *good* day?"

It was the dreaded question in our marriage for way too long. He dreaded it because he knew what I was really asking. I dreaded it because I was afraid of the answer. But the fear I had of the unknown was more than my fear of the answer. So I asked daily. Sometimes, if I was feeling especially disconnected from Luke, I'd ask multiple times a day. "How are you doing?" "Are you feeling tempted?" "What are you feeling right now?" "Are you having a hard time?" No matter how I worded it, we both knew what I was really asking. It became a wedge between us that kept him from opening up and kept me from feeling sane.

Wanting our spouse to share their feelings is normal and healthy. It's a powerful way to connect and is part of being attentive and attached. But it's only helpful and healthy if questions come from a place of genuine interest in and concern for the other person. That conversation might look something like this:

> Luke walks in the door after work, apathetically drops his bag, slams his body onto the couch, and immediately closes his eyes. I remember that he stayed up after I went to bed the night before. I leave the dishes I was washing in the sink, go over, and sit next to him. I place my hand on his back and start to rub. Picking up on his stress and fatigue, I know this is a surefire way to relax him. I feel the tension start to leave his body. I genuinely want to know what's on his mind so he doesn't have to feel that stress alone, so I say, "How was your day? You must be tired."

Now, compare that to this scenario:

> Luke walks in the door after work, apathetically drops his bag, slams his body onto the couch, and immediately closes his eyes. I stay at the sink where I'm doing the dishes and scrub harder, keeping my distance. I just know I'm about to be really hurt. I remember that he stayed up after I went to bed the night before. "He must have relapsed while I was asleep," I think to myself. "I knew he was going to." I'm now fuming. "I should never have gone to bed without him. He shouldn't have stayed up when no one else was awake. What was he thinking? What was I thinking? There he is just lying there. Is he even going to tell me?" I take a deep breath before moving the frustration from my head to my lips. Assuming he is about to confirm my fears, I try but fail to hide my accusation when I say, "How was your day? You must be tired."

One of the main differences between these two examples is trust.

A New Pattern of Honesty

When pornography is in a marriage, because betrayal has occurred and probably reoccurs, trust is going to be hard to come by. But trust can begin to be rebuilt, even when consistent sobriety hasn't been reached yet. It all starts with being honest.

I asked the dreaded question so much because I never knew if Luke was relapsing. Since I was left to worry and wonder, my fear convinced me that if he expressed anything remotely close to a negative emotion, he had already relapsed or was about to. It was a way I tried to brace myself for impact.

Our therapist helped identify this cycle and gave us some invitations. He invited Luke to be 100 percent transparent with the occurrences of his relapses. He invited me to not assume Luke had relapsed or that he was going to. I was supposed to trust that Luke would tell me if he did, even though the past taught me that he wouldn't.

It was going to be hard for us both. Luke would have to stand up to his shame that tells him to stay hidden after a relapse. I was going to have to stand up to my fear that tells me abandonment is always around the corner. It may be around some corners, but in truth, it wasn't around every corner. I needed to start allowing myself to feel the safety of the moments when Luke wasn't pulling away from me.

"This is the beginning of the road to rebuild trust," our therapist said, "but it will only work if you both do your side of it."

Luke and I looked at each other wondering what the other was thinking. Then Luke looked back at our therapist. "But when I tell her I relapsed, it hurts her so much. If I tell her *every time* . . . what will that do to her?"

"Luke, look what *not telling her* is doing to her! Look what it's doing to you both!"

We decided we would try our best. We first had to establish some expectations. We discussed how soon after a relapse he would tell me. There was some trial and error in figuring out how much about the relapse was helpful for him to share. It took time, patience, and effort, but eventually we got into a new pattern of honesty.

The results were amazing! Little by little, I started feeling a heavy burden lifted. I stopped being Luke's warden, which he and I were both grateful for. I felt liberated from the constant worry I had grown so used to.

It never got easier for Luke to tell me when he relapsed. He was still ashamed every time.

And I still had a lot of pain and fear. There was still that competing attachment within our marriage, so of course there were times when assumptions would fill my mind. But I learned to recognize them as assumptions instead of confirmed reality and treat them accordingly.

I'd remind myself that if Luke had relapsed, he would tell me. And if he hadn't told me, then he hadn't relapsed.

As oxygen started flowing between us again, I was able to share my fears with him in a much less crazy way. Instead of the dreaded question, I was able to say things like, "Luke, I'm worried that you relapsed without telling me. I'm not accusing you of lying or withholding anything. I guess I'm really just saying that I've felt disconnected from you today and I don't know why. You seem really distant, and I'm feeling a lot of fear about it."

With the changes in how I was communicating, Luke was able to hear my true underlying emotions that had been hiding behind all my nagging. He would do his best to respond in the same respectful and calm manner, without getting defensive, even if what I was saying was hard for him to hear. "I'm so glad you told me that you've been feeling disconnected and afraid, Elizabeth. I know that is really hard. Tell me more about what's been on your mind."

The purpose of that type of conversation wasn't to come up with a solution to my fear or for him to reassure me that he didn't relapse. It was about being vulnerable together and having that vulnerability be met with empathy. When that happened, my current fear was usually hushed by the attentiveness and stability that his empathy provided me with.

We established this pattern of honest disclosure years ago, and we still follow it today. I don't assume, and he doesn't hide.

And so, with the slow rebuilding of trust also came healthy communication and attachment. Trying to talk about our feelings used to be a wedge between us that fed disconnection. Now it's the very thing nurturing our bond.

9
I need to be careful too

BECAUSE OF PORNOGRAPHY, SHAME WAS A CONSTANT PRESENCE IN our little family for a long time. Luke and I both felt it. But what is shame exactly? It's an "intensely painful feeling or experience of believing that we are flawed and therefore unworthy of love and belonging—something we've experienced, done, or failed to do makes us [feel] unworthy of connection."[17] In reality, nothing can ever change our inherent worth. But shame bullies its victims into thinking that it can. Luke felt it because he was doing something he knew was wrong on many levels. I felt it because the person who was supposed to be my most stable earthly relationship was reaching for something other than me.

---

17. Brené Brown, "Shame vs. Guilt," Jan. 15, 2013, https://brenebrown.com/articles/2013/01/15/shame-v-guilt/.

Although Luke's unwanted pornography viewing was not really about sex or anything I lacked, intrusive thoughts of inadequacy and shame used to invade my thoughts on a daily basis.

"Does he keep looking at pornography because something is wrong with me? Am I not pretty enough? Sexy enough? Am I not good enough at sex?"

This internal, one-sided conversation snowballed into curiosity about what I was up against. Over time, curiosity turned into entitlement and became a toxic obsession. "I deserve to know what's destroying our marriage. I need to know exactly what he's seeing!"

Once, after several back-to-back relapses early in our marriage, these thoughts threw me into an emotional frenzy. I decided I would look back through the history on our devices to stare my opponent in the face. I thought it would either confirm whether I'm the problem or not.

Now, standing from the outside looking in, it really doesn't make sense. But in the moment, I felt like this was the answer to ending my turmoil, and I could think of nothing else.

Looking at pornography myself did confirm something for me, but it wasn't what I was expecting. It confirmed that I am *not* above the pull of temptation. No one is, except Jesus Christ.

At first, when I saw the kinds of things Luke was looking at, I was filled with disgust. I was completely repulsed. But that disgust turned into a very strong and scary sensation: pleasure.

This pleasure was followed by a wash of intense shame and loneliness. I felt like an absolute hypocrite. "No other girl on Earth, especially a wife who has been so hurt by pornography, has ever seen what I've seen and then felt what I've felt," I told myself. *"I'm* disgusting."

Later, when I was thinking a little more clearly, I realized that the cycle I had put myself in—a poor choice because of an intense emotion and an obsessive thought, leading to fake pleasure and ending in dark, suffocating shame—was probably exactly what Luke experienced every time he relapsed. It helped me understand him and gave me insight into his brokenness.

I took my poor choices to the Savior, and He was able to turn them into learning experiences, as only He can. It's a lesson I wish I would have learned in any other way. But now I knew—I could also be the one holding the grenade. Pornography is no respecter of persons.

10
I need to heal

I couldn't always see that when Luke relapses, it feels like he has caused an explosion to go off, and I'm hit by countless pieces of shrapnel. The pain of his choices let me know that I needed to heal, but I couldn't understand *what* needed to heal.

Even after doing therapy and learning about attachment and addiction, it was still so hard to wrap my head around my own trauma recovery. This probably had a lot to do with the fact that my pain would not only nag at me after one of Luke's relapses but also at what felt like random times in between those relapses. It seemed as if any healing that took place wasn't sticking.

I desperately wanted to make sense of our situation and see the big picture. I felt like I was always playing catch-up, trying to heal from past trauma with no clear idea as to what that really meant.

What was the goal? White-knuckled sobriety from him? Endless pain for me? Getting to a point in his recovery and my healing where we could pretend none of this happened? No, none of those felt right.

One Sunday afternoon, about eight years into our marriage, hopelessness overcame me. I was alone with my thoughts while putting clothes away in the kids' room.

Suddenly I completely fell apart. I collapsed onto the ground, knelt next to one of their toddler beds, and buried my sobbing face in the blankets. All I had the emotional strength to do was open up a prayer and continue crying in the embrace of my Heavenly Father.

I reflected on all that had unfolded in the previous months. I had embarked on a personal journey of health. I began to change my mindless relationship with food, learned how to properly fuel my body, and lost unhealthy weight. It was invigorating and exciting to feel good, to have energy, and to sleep well. Properly nourished, I felt like my body was able to function the way God had always intended. It felt incredible to be in control of my body and its urges.

I *really* wanted Luke to join me on that journey. I had seen how my physical health benefited every area of my life, so I tried to get him on board. But he was content with where he was at physically and always kindly and respectfully declined my invitations.

After a while, his complacency with his health really started to bother me. It was making me feel frustrated, hopeless, and afraid. It had nothing to do with his addiction, so why was it triggering my trauma response? These were the questions coming out with each tear as I knelt at my toddler's bed and cried.

Soon the Spirit connected the dots in my mind. We had been learning that a big part of addiction recovery is learning how to be mindful, meaning aware of what's happening in the mind. Mindfulness is knowing what you're feeling and thinking in the moment you're feeling and thinking it. It's a key component to acting as an agent instead of being acted upon by circumstances.

A desire to escape runs rampant in a state of mind*less*ness. If you aren't aware of what is going on inside you, then triggering emotions, situations, and thoughts can get out of hand and quickly lead you down unwanted paths. Just as getting physically healthy through mindfulness would improve other areas of Luke's life, I knew the opposite was also possible. I feared that his complacency and mindlessness with food would feed his temptation to view pornography as one escape feeding another.

So exerting all my energy, I pleaded for the Lord to help my husband discover a desire to be mindful. As I came to the very end of my emotional reservoir, these encouraging words came to me: "Elizabeth, I understand your concerns. Know that I am with you and I am with Luke. In your eyes, it has felt slow, but I have led you both along and will continue to do so. Soon your understanding will be opened and you will see. Continue in patience and faith."

Peace and comfort filled my soul. I didn't know how and I didn't know what, but I could feel it: Change was coming.

Eyes to See What Needs to Heal

Many months later, I was writing in my journal late one night to sort out my surfacing emotions. I was pondering on the many tender mercies that followed the prayer at my toddler's bed. With time, Luke did gain a desire to change his eating habits! He discovered the liberty associated with mindfulness. He was starting to have the confidence that comes from self-discipline. I loved it and so did he.

But what brought me to my journal that night was that despite Luke's new health habits, he had recently relapsed while away on a business trip. I was taking it incredibly hard because of all the change I had seen in him prior to his trip.

Fortunately, the Spirit took the pen and taught me through what I wrote. For the first time ever, I was able to see somewhat of a whole picture of what healing looks like.

> It's late, or maybe early. Too early. I can't sleep. I need to get out the things that are swirling around in my mind. Something is piecing itself together, but I can't quite put my finger on a complete idea just yet. I'm sure writing it out will help. It usually does.
>
> When I was going to therapy years ago to deal with Luke's addiction, I learned that what I experience is called betrayal trauma. The type of betrayal I deal with is traumatic because it destroys my sense of safety and attachment, which are basic survival needs. The relationship I hoped would be my safest place is now unpredictable and emotionally unsafe.

It's been going on very frequently for eight years of marriage now, and I think I can finally clearly see what that trauma response looks like for me.

Immediately after a relapse, I'm numb and don't want to see or talk to anyone. Then I start feeling a wide range of emotions. Those emotions are mostly expressed as a push and pull. I want to push Luke away and I want to pull him close to me. Sometimes I feel the push, sometimes the pull, and sometimes I feel both at the exact same time.

Even though he's the one who hurt me and disrupted my sense of stability, he's still the one I want to find comfort in and security with. To switch between so many different emotions—to feel many of them at the same time and to have them often be so conflicting—really heightens my anxiety. I struggle a lot with low confidence, which spills over to other areas of my life. I have panic attacks that usually occur at night as a result of being triggered by something that causes me to feel fear—fear that any stability I may feel at the time is going to be short-lived.

When Luke relapses, it feels like an explosion goes off. When I have what seems like a crazy emotion or reaction, it's like a piece of shrapnel from a previous explosion comes to the surface. Usually it takes a while after an explosion for these pieces of shrapnel to work their way to visibility.

Last night, I collected all the trash and was going to take it to the road to be picked up the following morning. It was late and Luke told me not to worry about it. He said he would do it in the morning before heading to work. Despite my worry that they would randomly come earlier than usual, he reassured me, "They never come before I leave for work. It'll be fine."

Well, this morning, for the first time since living here, they came way earlier than usual. Our trash is filled to the top and the thought of having no place to put next week's trash completely undid me.

Frustrated, I told Luke that they had come early. He looked confused as I started to cry—even more so as my crying turned to hyperventilating. My chest felt tight and I couldn't breathe. I was having a full-blown panic attack.

"I knew they would come—I knew it! I'm so dumb! Why did I trust you? I knew it, I knew it!" I kept saying over and over in my gasps for air.

Luke sat with me. He was kind and patient. But when it escalated to true panic, he sat me up, held my shoulders, and shook me. He said some things to try to help me see that it was going to be okay—it was just the trash.

I yanked myself out of his grip and yelled through my tears, "I knew it! I knew you would relapse on your trip! I'm so dumb! Why did I trust you? I knew it, I knew it!"

I fell onto the bed and pulled the covers over my head. He sat there with his hand on my back on top of the blanket while I cried.

After a long time, I slowly started to calm down until I was able to just lie there and breathe. I ended up falling asleep for a few minutes until Luke had to go to work. When I yelled about his relapse, I'm not sure who it surprised more, me or him. I wasn't sure where it came from, but it felt so good to get it out.

The trash can situation triggered my betrayal trauma. A piece of painful shrapnel had been working its way up since he relapsed and finally got to the surface this morning.

Luke's reaction was really beautiful and helpful. Through his empathy, he lovingly and carefully helped me remove that piece of shrapnel. I know it's difficult for him to do because every time I have a piece make its way to the surface, it causes him shame since he's the one who put it there in the first place.

There have been so many times in the past when he didn't respond with empathy. In those moments, when he has given into his shame by being defensive or shutting down as I express my heartache, it's like he has his hand on the piece of shrapnel that has worked its way to the surface, and instead of pulling it out, he pushes it back into my wound. It creates so much more damage. That piece still has to come out eventually and will resurface later. And when it does, it will be harder to heal from and all the more painful because of the damage that was caused as it was pushed back in.

When I share my emotions, even if it's in what seems like an irrational way, I'm trying to reach out for connection in a stable space with a secure person. Will he be that for me in that moment?

> *The initial explosion, of course, always makes me feel afraid. Then if he reacts with shame, it makes me feel more afraid. But when he owns what he did—when he responds with empathy and love and if he does that consistently over time—it adds to my sense of safety and trust. It contributes to my healing. And it goes both ways—I'm not the only one who has a body full of shrapnel. When he comes to me with a piece that has worked its way to the surface of his skin, I can do for him what I hope he does for me. This, combined with his efforts to detach from lust in all its forms, is the ultimate goal of healing our marriage.*
>
> *The hard part is that neither of us knows when a piece of shrapnel will surface. Neither of us knows how many pieces are in me from this explosion or from the hundreds that have occurred over the past eight years. But if a piece is never removed by him or by me or by the Lord or by some other person in a way that promotes healing, then that piece could stay there for years, fester, and get infected. I think that has occurred a lot over the course of our marriage, but for the first time in a long time, I feel really hopeful about the future because I understand what that future can look like.*

As I closed my journal, I laid down, amazed at the understanding that filled me. I could see Luke's efforts through the Lord's eyes. His newfound mindfulness was helping him to be empathetic, apply recovery skills, and access heaven's help.

It would be slow, but this was what the Lord had informed me of months prior. Luke's mind and heart were changing. The evidence was in how he responded to my surfacing shrapnel.

After so many years of receiving line upon line, I could now finally see the big picture of my own healing and that of my relationship with Luke. It was clear what my injuries looked like, what needed to heal, what my role was, and what Luke's role *could be* if he wanted to help mend our companionship.

11
I need support and connection

AFTER I UNDERSTOOD THE *WHAT* BEHIND MY HEALING PROCESS, I WAS then able to see the *how*—how to remove each piece of painful shrapnel. Because the danger and damage of lust lies in the disconnection it creates, the healing balm is connection. But how can a couple possibly connect when drowning in so much disconnection? The answer is empathy.

There are three parts to effective empathy:

- Seeing someone else's perspective without judgment
- Identifying the underlying emotion behind their perspective
- Communicating that back to them[18]

---

18. Theresa Wiseman, "A Concept Analysis of Empathy," *Journal of Advanced Nursing* 23, no. 6 (1996): 1162–67.

Empathy is recognizing that the emotion someone is feeling is real to them in that moment. It's feeling it with them so they don't have to feel it alone. Because this requires us to look outside of ourselves to clearly see another, showing empathy connects people.

Shame and empathy researcher Brené Brown found that connection is "the energy that exists between people when they feel seen, heard, and valued; when they can give and receive without judgment; and when they derive sustenance and strength from the relationship."[19] This is the goal of empathy, especially within a marriage where spouses feel cut off from one another. It's in the state of connection, which empathy provides, where the husband and wife can both feel stable enough and strong enough to work through their wounds. This is where lasting healing occurs.

Elaine Walton, the director of the BYU School of Social Work at the time, said the following in a devotional to emphasize the remarkable power of empathy:

> In supervising my students' beginning experiences as professional counselors, I find a common theme. Inexperienced counselors generally focus prematurely on identifying and solving the client's problem—such as failing grades, failing relationships, substance abuse, etc. These student counselors often come to supervision sessions frustrated—wondering why they can't get the client to recognize the problem, accept responsibility, or be motivated to change. As the student and I watch the videotape of the counseling session together, I find myself asking the same question over and over again: "What do you think the client is feeling right now?" As these novice counselors become more sensitized to the feelings of their clients and acquire skills in conveying that understanding with empathetic responses, we usually see progress. *We find that the clients—even those with the most profound problems—have remarkable*

---

19. Brené Brown, "Courage, Compassion, and Connection: The Gifts of Imperfection," Oprah.com, Mar. 12, 2013, https://www.oprah.com/own-super-soul-sunday/excerpt-the-gifts-of-imperfection-by-dr-brene-brown/all#ixzz5xqUCWyoG.

ability and motivation to change and to solve their own problems once they really feel understood.[20]

Jesus Christ provides the best example of empowering others through empathy. He shows us how to effectively be empathetic so that connection can occur even in a situation that seems impossible.

Think back to the account of Lazarus. When Lazarus died, his sisters, Mary and Martha, were understandably heartbroken. As soon as she could, Martha ran to the Savior with her sorrow. Together, Christ and Martha spoke of life, of death, and of resurrection.

Mary, however, stayed behind in her grief. Christ's ability to help Martha remember her own faith in Him comforted her so much that she ran back to their house to bring Mary to Him for that same comfort. After Mary heard from Martha that Jesus called for her—that He cared enough about what she was going through to want to be with her—she "arose quickly, and came unto him" (John 11:29).

> 32 Then when Mary was come where Jesus was, and saw him, she fell down at his feet, saying unto him, Lord, if thou hadst been here, my brother had not died.
>
> 33 When Jesus therefore saw her weeping, and the Jews also weeping which came with her, *he groaned in the spirit, and was troubled,*
>
> 34 And said, Where have ye laid him? They said unto him, Lord, come and see.
>
> 35 *Jesus wept.* (John 11:32–35; emphasis added)

Why did Christ not immediately teach and testify to Mary the way He did to Martha? He knew He was about to raise Lazarus from the dead—He said so to others earlier in the chapter. He could have told Mary, "You don't need to be so sad, Mary! I'm about to bring him back to life!"

But in His perfect example, He allowed Himself—the very one who was minutes from completely removing the source of Mary's sorrow—to feel what she was feeling in that moment. He recognized her brokenness. He understood that brokenness was her current focus,

---

20. Elaine Walton, "Empathy and the Pure Love of Christ" (Brigham Young University devotional, July 30, 2002), 3, speeches.byu.edu; emphasis added.

and He loved her enough to not minimize it. He didn't ignore the intensity of her pain with a quick fix or some encouraging words. He didn't try to convince her that there would be a happy ending. He took the time to understand her perspective and communicate that understanding back to her by weeping with her. It was only after doing this that He raised Lazarus from the dead.

Empathy is feeling with people. And feeling with people binds hearts together. It connects us. It strengthens us. It enables us and empowers us to move forward when overwhelmed with heavy, painful, difficult emotions, just as Mary was empowered to believe (see John 11:40). I can't read her encounter with the Savior without thinking of the many times He has seen my devastation and was troubled—when He has wept with me in my pain, especially concerning Luke's behavior to turn to sexual escape.

One by one, each piece of shrapnel, each wound, needs to be attended to. Unhealed pieces—or even worse, pieces that are harshly pushed back into the wound—*will* begin to fester and get infected. That infection can spiral out of control and spread to other areas of our lives very quickly.

But I have fantastic news! When people follow the Savior's example, the healing balm of empathy can come from a variety of sources, such as ecclesiastical leaders, friends and family, our husbands, and those on the other side of the veil. Believe it or not, we can even learn how to remove some of our own pieces (and we *need* to)! Finding these sources, though, does require a decent amount of risk.

******

Trying to find someone to open up to about my situation was scary. Hard. Almost impossible. Or at least that's how it felt for years.

Actually, the first time I tried was easy because it never crossed my mind that someone would respond to my heartache with anything but the empathy I needed. (I'm not sure why—I barely understood empathy myself at that point, and I quickly realized not many other people did either.) My search for empathy grew increasingly more difficult because of the walls I put up as a result of a few painful conversations.

Having said that, it really was never malicious or hateful. People's hurtful reactions usually had to do with either not knowing how to respond in a helpful way or being so distracted with their own trials and insecurities that they couldn't be there for me. Both are completely understandable but were isolating all the same.

The betrayal from my husband's struggle with sexual escape left me feeling raw, vulnerable, and not enough. In such a state, as Brené Brown said, "you can't call just anyone. If you share your shame story with the wrong person, he or she can easily become one more piece of flying debris in your already dangerous shame storm. We want solid connection in a situation like this—something akin to a sturdy tree firmly planted in the ground."[21]

So, who could I "call"?

Connecting with Ecclesiastical Leaders

When Luke and I were first married, he met with the bishop in our ward. He wanted to confess, seek forgiveness, and get help with his sexual sins.

I went with Luke. It was our first experience reaching out as a married couple for ecclesiastical support. I knew the bishop wasn't a therapist, but I thought he could guide me in my own *spiritual* healing throughout Luke's repentance process.

Unfortunately, he minimized the effect Luke's choices had on me, and in my naivety, I thought I was wrong for being hurt by Luke's actions. Looking back, it's clear now that that particular bishop probably didn't have much experience or training on how to handle the delicate situation. But neither did we.

And so, figuring he knew what he was talking about, I suppressed my pain and never reached out to him again. Come to think of it, neither did Luke.

******

---

21. Brené Brown, "Brené Brown: The Safe Way To Share Your Shame Story," HuffPost, Mar. 11, 2015, https://www.huffpost.com/entry/brene-brown-shame_n_4282679.

A few years later, I joined a Church-run addiction support group for wives. I learned that being hurt by my husband's repetitive sin was not an inappropriate response. I also learned I was not the only one who had painful experiences with ecclesiastical leaders.

I pondered on the many stories shared with me, as well as my own, and noticed something interesting. The times when bishops and stake presidents reacted in inappropriate ways seemed to fall near either end of a spectrum.

One end of the spectrum was being indifferent to wives when they sought out guidance and healing, like my first bishop did: "This is only between your husband and the Lord."

It's true that the main relationship that needs to be mended is indeed the relationship between our husbands and the Lord. However, it is *not* true that that is the only relationship that needs mending. And because the priesthood leader is called as a spiritual leader over both the husband and the wife, it is well within the leader's stewardship and ability to also provide spiritual guidance to the wife who is probably feeling like her connection to the Savior is on life support.

The other end of the spectrum finds leaders blaming wives for their husband's actions. "Well, are you doing enough to meet his sexual needs?"

Another example of this was our stake president, who acknowledged my painful heartbreak but then said I had my head in the sand and needed to be more strict in expecting absolute sobriety, as if the outcome of Luke's recovery was in my hands.

Without excusing their incorrect messages, it's important to differentiate *their* reaction—men who are human, imperfect, and just doing the best they can with the knowledge they have—from *the Lord's* reaction. Jesus Christ is perfect and is the same yesterday, today, and forever (see Moroni 10:19; Mormon 9:9). Looking at how He reacted to this sin "yesterday" can help us know how He still feels today.

In the Book of Mormon, the Savior had His prophet Jacob speak to Church members about breaking the law of chastity: "For behold, I, the Lord, have seen the sorrow, and heard the mourning of the daughters of my people in the land of Jerusalem, yea, and in all the lands of my people, because of the wickedness and abominations of their husbands. . . . Ye have broken the hearts of your tender wives, and lost the confidence of your children, because of your bad examples before them; and the sobbings of their hearts ascend up to God against you" (Jacob 2:31, 35; emphasis added).

The Savior has always been very aware of the wife's side of this story. He wants His disciples to portray that in their ministering efforts. He counsels them to "express [their] love and concern for her individually, as well as for her spouse. Clarify that she is not responsible for her spouse's pornography use or poor behavior and is not expected to endure abusive behavior."[22]

One bishop shared some of the things he has learned from counseling couples who have had pornography afflict their marriages. He wrote:

> Because it is the husband who has transgressed, it is easy for the bishop to feel that the husband most needs access to the keys to unlock the Savior's healing power, but I have learned that the wife's need to be healed of pain and trauma is as great as the husband's need to be healed of sin and obsessive urges. . . .
>
> I have learned that the counsel to minister to the wives is inspired. I hope that no sister in this situation will ever feel that she is being overlooked, misjudged, or misunderstood by her bishop. The bishop's ministration is a key channel through which the Savior manifests His power to fully heal each heart—even those that have been "pierced with deep wounds" (Jacob 2:35).[23]

Take heart, dear wife. As shown in the above testimony, not all leaders will react with one of these extremes. It is my personal belief that the spiritual leaders who are or have been at either end of this spectrum are there unbeknownst to them. And as the topics of pornography, lust, sexual escape, and masturbation become more understood among members of the Church (and less taboo), I believe we will find that spectrum and those extremes disappear altogether.

---

22. "When Pornography Hits Home—Wives and Husbands Both Need to Heal," *Ensign*, Apr. 2016, 39.
23. "When Pornography Hits Home," 39.

******

Years after my experience with that first bishop, we ended up moving to another state for graduate school. Luke met with our new bishop regularly on his quest for a change of heart and seemed completely filled with the love of God after each time they met. He always came out of the bishop's office with a brighter light in his eyes than he had when he went in. I desperately wanted that too.

After going to therapy, I understood my trauma from a temporal standpoint, but now I wanted to understand it spiritually. I wanted to talk to someone who could counsel me concerning the covenant I had made in the temple with Luke, who knew Luke's heart, and who had authority to speak on behalf of the Savior. So I set up an appointment.

When the time came for us to meet, I left Luke to put our toddler to bed and drove to the church building. I was pregnant enough with our second child that the steering wheel in our tiny car rubbed against my belly as I got in. I put some music on to distract me from how nervous I was.

Because of my previous experience, I worried the whole time that he would think I was overreacting and dramatic. I was also afraid it would make him feel uncomfortable and awkward.

That's the scariest part of opening up to someone about this—you don't know how they'll respond until they actually respond. But by that time, you can't undo what you've said, so you just hold your breath and hope they were a good person to share such hard things with. Many wives, including myself, have stayed hidden in the shadows of their husband's inappropriate sexual behaviors for fear of the unknown reactions of others.

When I got to the church building, I parked, took a deep breath, and said a prayer that all would go well. I prayed for courage. I prayed for strength. I prayed that my heartache would be received with empathy. I got out of my car and walked into the building. The bishop saw me, shook my hand, and invited me into his office. We talked for a bit, then he asked what he could do for me. I took the leap, told him my story, and held my breath.

He sat there silently looking at me. The love that filled his eyes brought tears to mine as I breathed a sigh of relief. Before he even said anything, I could tell that this was the ecclesiastical empathy I had longed for, for so long.

I realized in this comfortable silence that he was listening to the Spirit to know what to say. After some time, and trying to hold back tears of his own, he said, "Sister Wells, I'm so glad you shared this with me." Tears rolled down my cheeks. He heard me *and I still mattered.*

"Our Savior Jesus Christ knows of your pains and fears," he continued. "He appreciates your efforts to be close to Him, and He is with you." He shared uplifting messages from the scriptures that fed my hungered soul.

It's interesting—he never told me anything the Holy Ghost hadn't already personally taught me throughout the years of being married to Luke. He also didn't try to fix anything or act as a therapist. He listened. He empathized. He loved. He testified. He invited. He ministered to me and counseled with me, I believe, as the Savior would have.

We ended with a prayer and I walked out smiling. I understood why Luke always left his office feeling the way he did. His vulnerability was met with Christlike compassion.

Now mine was too.

Connecting with Family and Friends

Family and friends can be a great source of very powerful empathy because of the established relationship they have with the couple. Often, these are the people wives want to be able to talk to the most. That meaningful relationship is also the reason non-empathetic family and friends can be so damaging. But why would loved ones respond in painful ways? One reason is because of the comfort level they have with the couple. While good-intentioned, sometimes the love they have can blur the line of what's actually helpful. They can try to play the role of a therapist or mediator instead of solely being a stable place to just let the couple hurt. Taking on the couple's burden isn't helpful or healthy for anyone.

Another reason is that they don't understand the severity of the situation and therefore don't realize how important their support is. While probably meant to comfort the wife, or perhaps cope with *their own discomfort* discussing pornography, the temptation to pat her on the back with a quick "Oh, it'll all work out" and then change the subject only tells her that she should never bring it up again.

I also found that the reactions of family and friends could be so heartbreaking if they weren't empathetic because I cared what they thought of me and Luke—especially what they thought of Luke. It's one of the main reasons I was private about this part of my life for so long, particularly with my own family. I didn't want anyone's opinion of Luke to change. I was terrified they would judge him without understanding his side, his efforts, and his wounds. I was also working incredibly hard to do the Lord's will, and I worried that if their opinions about Luke (or the decisions they thought I should make in my struggling marriage) weren't in line with His, it would muddy the waters I was trying to wade through. My worry and fear fed my isolation and kept it alive.

Many years ago, one of my closest friends and I were talking. She didn't know anything about Luke's affliction or the struggles we had in our marriage. I always wanted to tell her, but I was never sure how she would react.

During this particular conversation, she told me about a friend of hers who recently told her that her husband had a pornography problem. It was obvious she felt for her friend, and a spark of hope filled me. Maybe I could tell her too!

Just as I was about to share my story, she said, "Man, I just feel bad for her, you know? How could he do such an awful thing to her! Doesn't it make you so glad our husbands don't struggle with that?"

Completely deflated, the word "yeah" was all I could muster up the courage to say.

******

Someone I could talk to without her opinion of Luke changing was his mom. Luke told his parents about his struggles, so it was helpful that when I talked to her about it, it didn't catch her off guard.

I remember one conversation in particular that was especially healing for me. Luke and I were visiting his parents over a long weekend. There was an afternoon when his mom and I were the only ones in the house. She very thoughtfully took that opportunity to ask specifically how I was doing. Luke had recently reached out to his dad for support, so she knew I had to be hurting too. I appreciated her asking. It made me feel like I wasn't a forgotten piece in the puzzle of her son's recovery.

So I told her about Luke's recent relapses and how I was feeling. We started our conversation standing in the hallway, leaning against the wall. As I dug further and further into my very fresh wound to grab hold of a particularly painful piece of shrapnel, we both lowered to the floor and sat across from each other. When I finished, she had tears in her eyes. She struggled to get her words out.

"Elizabeth, I love my son. I know that he will one day conquer this. But that doesn't change the reality of the pain and the damage his choices are causing right now. You are hurting so much. I would be too. I can never think about his choices without also thinking about you—without thinking about what it forces you to face. You are just so strong."

We were both in tears now, and as we hugged, I reflected on why I felt so good. She heard what I was feeling *underneath* the situation of Luke's relapses and acknowledged the difficulty I endured on many levels. How I was feeling was her focus.

Because she had taken the initiative in her own time to learn about "pornography addiction," she could focus on my feelings when we talked instead of the circumstances surrounding them. She didn't press me for details on what happened, and I didn't have to stop in the middle of pouring my broken heart out to explain what certain recovery-related terms, ideas, or issues meant. At that time, I didn't have the emotional energy to teach her or anyone else about the things Luke and I had learned from therapy and personal study over the years. I needed someone who already understood a little about where I was coming from when I came to them in my pain. And really, so did Luke. We didn't expect them to understand on a professional level, but we needed someone whose simple efforts would make sharing our feelings not so draining.

Luke's parents became those types of people for us. They were able to support us like few others could. Their humility and dedication remind me of the prophet Isaiah when the Lord asked who He should send to serve His people. Who could be His hands? Someone ready and willing to support His children as He would. Without fully understanding the complexity and details of the service needed, Isaiah humbly and meekly answered, "Here am I; send me" (Isaiah 6:8).

Luke's parents probably still don't fully understand the complexity and details of our situation or how their support has been helpful. But they've tried their best to be humble (learning from God) and to also be meek (learning from other people)[24] about "pornography addiction" and recovery.

Sometimes I picture Heavenly Father receiving prayers of heartache from so many. And as He ponders who He should send as His hands to their aid, He sees the humble and meek efforts of people like Luke's parents. He sees them study, learn, read, listen, pray, fast, and ask. But really what He sees in those efforts echoes what He has heard in days long passed: "Here am I; send me."

Grateful that she learned about such a difficult topic when it wasn't even her personal trial, I continued to reflect on other reasons why talking with Luke's mom helped so much. She didn't minimize the pain Luke or I felt, and yet she also wasn't shocked, disappointed, or dramatic about it either. She didn't seem squeamish or uncomfortable. She didn't try to make me feel better instantly or fix anything. In fact, she didn't give me any advice. She also understood that I could be frustrated and hopeless and so, so hurt by Luke *and* still love him. She didn't even ask me why I said a certain thing or felt a certain way. She listened. As Jesus Christ did with Lazarus's sister, Mary, she allowed herself to feel the pain I was expressing so that, in that moment, I didn't have to feel it alone. And when I moved on to a different

---

24. See David A. Bednar, "Meek and Lowly of Heart," *Ensign* or *Liahona*, May 2018, 30–33.

emotion, she moved along with me. This allowed me to be raw and confused and to be okay not being okay.

******

Each time I felt heard and was able to express my pain with my mother-in-law, with my bishop, and with other empathetic family and friends, I was in a better place to receive the healing power of Jesus Christ and see His hand in my life and Luke's life.

Like Mary, only after receiving empathy did I feel capable of following Christ to the tomb my husband's affliction had laid him in. I was able to look past my own grief and watch the Redeemer slowly bring not only Luke back to life, little by little, but also our marriage. Like Mary, I was truly empowered to "see the glory of God" (John 11:40).

This is the opportunity, the privilege, the calling for *all* who wish to be stable, empathetic people to those who suffer. We've been told that if we have the desire, we are called to the Lord's work (see Doctrine and Covenants 4:3). How we respond to that call is in our hands. "Therefore, dearly beloved brethren, let us cheerfully *do all things that lie in our power*" (Doctrine and Covenants 123:17; emphasis added).

Connecting with Myself

"[Stress is] the mind wanting things to be different from how they are. It can arrive quickly and unexpectedly, momentarily throwing you off balance. Or it can build more slowly, taking longer to pass."[25] No matter how quickly they come, or how long they take to pass, the stress-inducing pieces of shrapnel within us *will* reach the surface at some point.

It was difficult, but I learned the empowering truth that I could remove some of those pieces—and not only that I *could* but that I *needed* to. After Luke would tell me he viewed pornography, if I didn't connect with myself first, oftentimes the things people would say to

---

25. "Stress 101," Headspace, accessed Aug. 22, 2024, https://www.headspace.com/stress/stress-101.

support me fell on deaf ears. I just wouldn't be in the right frame of mind to receive their help.

We are all unique, so how we connect with ourselves may look different. For example, you could immerse yourself in nature, exercise, go to the temple, get a massage, practice deep breathing, write in your journal, go for a walk, do a craft, knit, or take a bubble bath. Whatever you do, find something that will allow you to *show yourself empathy,* or in other words, *feel and reflect.* That means finding a place or activity where you can:

- See your perspective (thoughts, desires, motivations) without judgment
- Identify the underlying emotion(s) behind your perspective
- Communicate that understanding back to yourself

We need to accept the discomforts we can't control, even though ignoring them or trying to change them may be the easier choice. Something I had to watch out for when deciding how to connect with myself was any type of activity that tempted me to binge, like watching shows, eating, shopping, or scrolling. These seemed rejuvenating on the surface but always ended up doing more harm than good. They would distract me from contemplating my feelings and leave me feeling worse about myself.

Instead, what I really needed was to allow my thoughts and feelings to come, observe them, learn from them, and watch them pass by. This does take effort, so years ago, I started practicing meditation as a way to train my mind to more naturally put forth that effort. As I did, I learned this amazingly helpful concept:

> Training the mind is often quite different than how people imagined it to be. Maybe they have an idea it's about stopping thoughts or eliminating feelings. But the reality is a bit different. An easy way to think of it is to imagine yourself sitting on the side of a busy road, the passing cars representing thoughts and feelings. All you have to do is just sit there and watch the cars. Sounds easy, right? But what usually happens is that we feel a bit unsettled by the movement of the traffic. So we run out into the road and try to stop the cars. Or maybe even chase after a few, forgetting that the idea

was to just sit here. And of course, all of this running around only adds to the feeling of restlessness in the mind. So training the mind is about changing our relationship with the passing thoughts and feelings. Learning how to view them with a little more perspective. And when we do this, we naturally find a place of calm. Will we sometimes forget the idea of the exercise and become distracted? Of course we will. But as soon as we remember, here we are, back on the side of the road again, just watching the traffic go by, perfectly at ease in both body and mind.[26]

Watching My Cars Pass to Obtain Peace

I keep a journal. It's one of my favorite ways to connect with myself. I don't, however, keep a journaling schedule that says I need to write this often or that often. I also don't worry about whether or not my posterity will one day read the things I record.

Sometimes my entries are a sentence or two. Sometimes they're pages long. I try not to pressure myself with "have-tos" or rigidity when it comes to writing. My journal is simply about coming to understand myself and allowing the Spirit to help me see my life more clearly.

It's the perfect place to celebrate sweet moments, sacred experiences, and funny things my kids say. I also use it to process my feelings when something seems off internally, when negativity is nagging at me, or when I feel numb. Whether those difficult experiences have to do with Luke's choices or not, writing out my vulnerabilities to see them through an observer's lens gives me a wider perspective.

It's also strengthening to go back and reread journal entries, especially after Luke gives into sexual escape. Doing so helps me to step outside my current situation and reminds me there is more to me and my life than the pain I feel. They provide me with evidence that I'm capable of happiness, healing, and peace. There have been times when the only strain of hope I had in the aftermath of an explosion

---

26. Headspace, "Quick Meditation: Changing Perspective," YouTube video, Aug. 18, 2017, https://youtu.be/iN6g2mr0p3Q?si=gU3I5EuZ-BMjngO3.

was from seeing myself make it through previous relapses, along with other trials, throughout the pages of my journal.

At the beginning of an entry meant to help me process my feelings, I may write down everything I have bottled up. Or I may not know what I'm feeling and just start writing any words that come to mind and then go from there. Something I've found very helpful in this regard has been the Feelings Wheel, designed by Dr. Gloria Willcox in 1982.[27] Many different versions of the original Feelings Wheel have since been created, and you can find a link to my favorite one in the corresponding footnote or by scanning the following QR code.[28]

One of the most difficult parts of understanding our own emotions is to put a name to them. The Feelings Wheel has helped me do this (and it's helped Luke too for that matter). To use it, start at the middle of the circle and identify the feeling you are having—surprised, happy, sad, disgusted, angry, fearful, or bad. Then follow that to the next ring of listed emotions. Keep identifying through to the last ring. Repeat this until you have named everything you are feeling. Say them out loud, write them down, or share them with your husband, a trusted loved one, or Heavenly Father in prayer. You can do this about the present moment or about the past, like before bed as you look back on your day.

---

27. Gloria Willcox, "The Feeling Wheel: A Tool for Expanding Awareness of Emotions and Increasing Spontaneity and Intimacy," *Transactional Analysis Journal* 12, no. 4 (2017): 274–276. https://doi.org/10.1177/036215378201200411

28. "I Feel - Emotional Word Wheel - The Feel Wheel," Imgur, Mar. 5, 2015, https://imgur.com/gallery/i-feel-emotional-word-wheel-feel-wheel-tCWChf6.

Give this a try sometime soon. Believe me, it's easier said than done, but the more you practice being able to name what you're feeling, the better you'll get at it.

If I'm prayerful, by the middle of the journal entry, I have a better idea of what my true feelings are. And by the end, a lot of times I've reached peace on that particular matter or emotion, even though the circumstances surrounding my feelings didn't change. There is such power in being able to shift our perspective, especially when we can't change our circumstances. If, however, by the end of the entry I still didn't feel peace, then at the very least, I felt heard. Feeling heard is usually a prerequisite to peace for me, so that journal entry set me up to feel peace at some point in the future.

Relapses are so disorienting. As the wife, it feels like the ground slips right out from under you and there's nothing you can do about it. But it's empowering to know our own mind and heart. When we do, we can at least have control over that—not control over *what* we feel but rather control over *how we respond* to what we feel. When I connect with myself—when I can identify my thoughts and feelings and allow myself to feel them and then let them pass like cars in traffic—I gain back some control in the chaotic situation I've been thrown into. I am then able to act instead of being acted upon by my circumstances or the ever-changing thoughts and emotions inside me.

With time and practice, I was able to identify all the feelings that stemmed from betrayal without judging them in the moment, without allowing them to hijack how I saw myself and my situation, and without letting them be the only factor in the decisions I made.

We need to be able to feel without immediately reacting in permanence. We need to give ourselves time to let the dust settle before we start trusting the thoughts that come, because when we are in a state of pain, panic, or numbness, our vision is so distorted.

I've learned I can feel pain without letting it define me. I can feel hopeless without giving up. I can feel sad or betrayed or lonely without losing my sense of self-worth. I can let my feelings be just that: feelings—things I feel in the moment and that's all. The Apostle Paul taught about this type of perspective when he said, "We are troubled on every side, yet not distressed; we are perplexed, but not in despair; persecuted, but not forsaken; cast down, but not destroyed" (2 Corinthians 4:8–9).

I've seen that when I am gasping for oxygen post-explosion, scraping at the rubble with bloody, shrapnel-filled hands for someone to help, I can be so overcome with my current storm of emotions that I overlook how much power and strength I have to *help myself*. We have the ability to show ourselves empathy. We *need* to show ourselves empathy. It is in this grounded frame of mind—which comes from being heard without being judged, even by our own selves—that we can move forward toward understanding, healing, and yes, even peace.

Peaceful Alone Time? Yeah, Right—I'm a Mom

I remember having an especially rejuvenating experience one morning while doing yoga and meditation, which are two ways I enjoy slowing down and connecting with myself. I got on my knees and bowed forward for one of the first positions, Child's Pose. I stretched out my arms and placed my palms on the floor in front of me. As soon as my forehead hit the ground and relaxed, I saw myself through heaven's eyes and was connecting with the eternal, divine part of myself. I was not expecting that! Nevertheless, it was a very welcome surprise.

With time, my toddlers came into the room as I changed to Easy Pose for the five-minute meditation portion. Usually they hang all over me in each yoga position like I'm a jungle gym, but I figured they would find me uninteresting in this simple crisscross-applesauce sitting pose. Yeah, I was dead wrong. One of my daughters stood in front of me for almost the entire five minutes, poking my closed eyes and saying with very pancake-syrup-smelling breath, "Eyes. Eyes. Eyes. Eyes."

Allowing myself to feel the humor of the moment instead of being annoyed by the interruption, I smiled and was filled with joy. I realized that the Lord can use my interactions with my kids—since they're the ones who usually disrupt my *me time*—to be a source of connection, happiness, and healing. I also was amazed to realize He can still help me connect with my inner peace even if it's during pockets of time amid the silliness, noise, and tantrums of life as a mom. It may just require a mental shift to that wider perspective. In fact, it's only by metaphorically sitting on the side of the road, watching my toddlers' interruptions as if they were cars passing by, that I'm able to see them for what they really are: innocent, loving "bids for connection"[29] with me.

When done in humility, things like temple attendance, meditation, prayer (which is a type of meditation), and scripture study, even when interrupted, are meant to show us the eternal pattern of peace—what it feels like, how to recognize it, and how to help it flourish. As I became familiar with peace, I discovered it in other places throughout my daily life as well. All things really are spiritual (see Doctrine and Covenants 29:34), and peace is hidden everywhere. But too often we're distracted or inexperienced with peace and we miss it.

I understand a little more now why God invites us to be still (see Psalm 46:10)—so He can teach us what peace feels like and remind us that it is most certainly attainable every day. Even when laden with heavy burdens. Even if shrapnel is surfacing. Even if tiny, sticky fingers are repeatedly poking us in the eyes as we try to connect with ourselves. Peace is ours for the taking. Will we take it?

Connecting with My Husband

> It's morning. And even though the sun is shining, dark clouds are lingering inside me. I've started moving away from the phase of "feeling numb the first day after Luke relapses" and have moved into an intense angry phase. I want to send him a message expressing my anger and annoyance and frustration and pain, but I also don't want to make him feel bad. But I sort of do. But I also don't. But I really do. Maybe if I get it out here first, I'll be able to have more clarity on what to do.
>
> Why did you have to relapse?! I specifically told you I was anxious you would before you left for your trip! You told me you were scared you would too. So did you do anything to prevent it or be on guard at all? I mean it's like you relapsed the first chance you had! The last several times we've been apart, you've relapsed

---

29. See Ellie Lisitsa, "Dr. Gottman's Guide to Recognizing Bids," The Gottman Institute, last modified Mar. 4, 2024, https://www.gottman.com/blog/self-care-friendship-and-dr-gottmans-guide-to-recognizing-bids/.

the first night! Were you looking forward to it when you closed the door of the hotel room and realized you could look at pornography? Were you glad to finally be alone? Did the kids and I even enter your mind?

I'm torn. I hope we did because I want us to be your priority, but then again, I hope you didn't think about us, about me, because that means you dismissed the thought of how much relapsing would hurt us. Maybe your addict whispered to you, "It's fine, it's not that bad—she'll forgive you afterward." So which is it? Did you not have us at the forefront of your mind, or did you but dismissed the thought? Either way, it's prideful and selfish, which just isn't you at all! You aren't prideful and selfish, but you did do a very prideful and selfish thing!

I mean, you had to know how much harder it would make things on me when I'm already having a hard weekend alone with sick kids. Now I'm even more on my own, left to handle everything by myself as best I can, trying to not let my pain affect the kids. But I'm not that strong and it always does. It affects them and it affects me. That's what happens when you relapse, Luke—you separate yourself from us and from the Lord. Do you feel it? You turn your focus away from us to get a few moments of instant gratification that actually never end up satisfying!

You need to make a choice—do you want to be married to pornography or do you want to be married to me? Do you want to be intimate with pornography or do you want to be intimate with me? Because you cannot be with both. Intimacy is based on safety and trust, and those have been severed so many times! I will say that the thing I *do* trust is that you *will* relapse the first night after we are ever apart because that is what has been consistent time and time again.

I do also trust that you will be sorry and repentant afterward too. That is also consistent, which I'm grateful for, really. But at least from where I'm sitting, that intense desire to never let it happen again seems to fade over time. How do you think it's going in between relapses to work toward breaking this cycle? Especially knowing a trip was coming up! Honestly, ask yourself if that's how you would have worked your recovery if your marriage depended on it—if your *life* depended on it. Because both do, Luke, and I don't feel like you realize that.

It's night now and I'm back here, writing in my isolation. I ended up waiting the whole day and thinking over my feelings without sending all that to him. I mean, when he told me he relapsed, he told me that he wanted to know how I was feeling and that whenever I was ready to share my feelings, he wanted me to. Well, tonight Annie [our toddler daughter] peed on the couch and it was the last straw—I completely lost it. I yelled at her and was being so controlled by my anger toward Luke that I just went to my phone and texted him what I wrote in here earlier. I apologized to Annie a little later and never heard from Luke. He didn't answer when the kids called to say goodnight, so they left him a message. Thinking the missed call was from me and not the kids, he texted and said he didn't want to talk right now because he was feeling really defensive. What? Seriously? He tells me to open up about my feelings and then gets defensive and shuts down when I do? I understand he's stressed with work, and I understand he's trying to focus on his training there in Cleveland—then don't relapse! If you don't want the added stress and burden of a heartbroken wife, then don't break her heart!

I emailed [my therapist] yesterday to see about starting couples therapy again. I feel like we could really benefit from that direction and structure in our recovery and healing efforts. I know he's busy, but I would really love to just talk to someone about this, you know?

I feel incredibly alone in my pain, fear, confusion, and anxiety. I should talk with my Heavenly Father about it more often. Writing in a journal does help. I feel less alone, like someone is listening as I write out my innermost thoughts and feelings. And it's actually really amazing to have a safe place to go to in my journal where I can talk without fear of judgment or feeling like I have to choose my words carefully.

When I write, I also feel like I'm not inconveniencing anyone, which is one reason I don't reach out to others about this. The main reason I don't, though, is because I've had a lot of negative experiences in the past with reaching out for support about Luke's sex addiction with family and friends. It rarely has gone well, and when it has gone well, it didn't seem to help me. Take Grace [a friend] for example. It goes well talking with her, but I'm almost scared to delve deep into my feelings because, for one, I don't want

> to trigger her since she's in the middle of a separation due to her own husband's sex addiction, and two, she isn't healed and so I feel like sometimes her advice is coming from a place of pain (which is completely understandable). What I need, though, is someone who has been through this betrayal and is on the other side of it. But everyone I know who is struggling with this is still in the struggle. It would be the blind leading the blind.
>
> Whether others can support me or not shouldn't matter though because to be perfectly honest, the person I want support from the most is Luke. He's the one I want to connect with. He's the one I want to reassure me and love me and care for me. He's the one I want to listen to me and sit with me while I cry, even though he's the one who made me cry. There's that push-and-pull thing again. I'm so hurt when he shuts down or gets defensive like he's doing right now. When he isn't there for me in these moments, it feels like more damage is done to my trust and to our relationship than even a relapse causes. I just feel so abandoned tonight from him shutting down when I reached out for him. It's causing me so much fear about the state of our marriage because I flat-out told him these things as yet another bid for connection, and he still hasn't responded. How could he do this to me?

Giving into sexual escape always leads to loneliness and disconnection. When Luke and I started consistently sharing these and other feelings with one another, it helped us start to reconnect instead of letting the relapse come between us. But this was not easy, as shown in the above journal entry, and often felt like a very tall order.

Sometimes we would have to remind each other and ourselves that the enemy is pornography, not the other person. It's an intruder in the marriage that couples can attack together by showing each other empathy. We were surprised to discover how much hard work and practice this takes. We're still not perfect at communicating our feelings effectively and that's okay. As long as we continue to try, that in and of itself shows that we *want* to connect with each other, which keeps our hearts soft and selfless.

Yin and Yang, Not Yin and Yin

What was really going on in that journal entry was a situation that used to happen a lot, especially in the beginning: Luke would be so overcome with feeling bad about himself after a relapse that it was hard for him to face the fact that he made me feel bad too. And the times when he did feel like he could listen to my hard feelings, he wouldn't ask because he thought I didn't want him to since he was the one who caused my pain. He figured I wanted him to just go away, so that's what he would do. Sometimes, on the surface, I did want that in my initial traumatic reaction. But deep down, I wanted him to stay as close as possible to show me he really wasn't abandoning me or our covenants.

When I learned that these things were going on in his mind, I knew we needed to get on the same page. I waited for a time in between relapses when he wasn't overcome by his shame. "Luke," I said one evening, "when you relapse, it makes me feel far away from you. Then when you don't ask about my pain or want to hear my feelings, it seems like you don't care about me or care that what you did affects me. It makes me feel even worse and further away from you. Even though it's your relapsing that hurts me, you're still my best friend; you're still the one I want to comfort me in this. Most times, I really just want you to stay with me while I process what has happened. You can't fix anything in that moment, so you don't need to try. But you *can* be with me so that I don't have to cry alone."

After he understood that—which took a lot of reminding, reiterating, and patience on my part and so much humility on his part—he began to stay with me physically and emotionally in the aftermath of relapses. This was exactly what I needed. Him remaining present without judging me, shaming me, shaming himself, minimizing the situation, trying to make it better, or turning the focus back to himself reassured me that even though there is this other thing competing for his primary attachment, he really does want that attachment to be with me.

This was liberating. Once he heard my heartache and still wanted to stay with me in it, my focus would turn to him. I wanted to honestly understand and empathize with the pain his relapse caused *him*. Over time, we started empathizing with each other. It was hard because we both had to listen and feel one another's underlying emotions without being overcome by our own feelings in that moment. We had to keep our focus on the other person, trusting that our time to be heard would come.

Sometimes Luke would revert back. He would ask me how I was feeling, but then when I told him, he would shut down because he was so ashamed, like he did when he was in Cleveland. He'd blame himself and I would have to lean into compassion to calmly say, "Luke, you're withdrawing again, right now. Please stay with me. I know it's hard to hear how I feel when you relapse, but you hearing these things and still comforting me tells me that I'm important to you." Being calm was key. I couldn't meet his defensiveness with my own, otherwise the whole conversation would blow up. But this is not a unique concept. It's like this with many things in a relationship, isn't it? When one person is struggling to have perspective on any topic, if the other is intentional and calm about how they handle the situation, they can help the other see more clearly. It's yin and yang, not yin and yin!

What If He Isn't Humble?

When you clean a cut, it hurts. The pain, however, does not mean that the cleaning process needs to stop. Cleaning has to happen for proper healing to occur. The one looking at pornography needs to understand and feel the natural consequences of his choices, even if it hurts, so that his metaphorical cuts can be completely cleansed. He also has to remain connected through those painful consequences so that the marriage can be cleansed and healed as well.

The goal is that with time, he will overcome the temptation to run away from this pain and from focusing on what his shame is telling him—"I'm such an idiot for making her feel so bad!" or "She's overreacting!" Instead, the goal is for him to respond to her feelings with true Christlike empathy and love—"She's feeling really scared. I know what feeling scared is like. I'll stay present with her so she doesn't have to feel it alone."

Even though it was uncomfortable for Luke, when he honestly acknowledged my feelings and took responsibility for his actions by looking outside of himself, he helped remove some of my shrapnel as well as some of his own.

I used to think the restitution part of repentance was about making the person we hurt feel better by removing their pain. It's not, because we can't! Just like it's not my role to fix Luke's behaviors of escape, it's not his role to fix my heartache, even though it's his actions that caused it. *He doesn't have the capacity to.* Referencing Alma's sinful choices and similar dilemma, President Boyd K. Packer said:

> There are times you cannot mend that which you have broken. . . . Perhaps the damage was so severe that you cannot fix it no matter how desperately you want to.
>
> Your repentance cannot be accepted unless there is a restitution. If you cannot undo what you have done, you are trapped. It is easy to understand how helpless and hopeless you then feel and why you might want to give up, just as Alma did.
>
> The thought that rescued Alma, when he acted upon it, is this: Restoring what you cannot restore, healing the wound you cannot heal, fixing that which you broke and you cannot fix is the very purpose of the atonement of Christ.
>
> When your desire is firm and you are willing to pay the "uttermost farthing," the law of restitution is suspended. Your obligation is transferred to the Lord. He will settle your accounts.[30]

The restitution part of Luke's repentance process is about putting aside his own pain and acknowledging another's, then doing all he can to humbly activate and rely on the restorative abilities of Jesus Christ. With this knowledge, it's clear that the purpose of connecting with Luke isn't for him to fix my broken heart. That's the Savior's role. The purpose is for him to *feel* my broken heart—for us to feel each other's.

This process of turning outward is refining. It gives him the opportunity to watch the Savior create beauty in the ashes of his explosive

---

30. Boyd K. Packer, "The Brilliant Morning of Forgiveness," *Ensign*, Nov. 1995, 19–20.

choices and extinguish the fire of shame burning within himself. If he allows it to, this can inspire him to live like the very One who is "healing the wounds [he] cannot heal." As he puts that desire into action, he can come to "have no more disposition to do evil, but to do good continually" (Mosiah 5:2) and to be "clean every whit" (John 13:10).

Like Alma's softening, your husband's may require fasting and prayer "with much faith" on the part of his loved ones as well as miraculous divine intervention (Mosiah 27:14). But the Lord has shown us time and time again that such a softening is possible.

So, dear wife, *do not give up* if at first your husband pushes against your efforts to connect with him. We all cringe at and perhaps resist the cleaning of our physical wounds, especially at first. It hurts. So it can be with our spiritual wounds. But eventually, he can get to the point that when he sees the Savior comforting you—and also, with time, when he sees *himself* comforting you—it will be naturally comforting for him. His heart can then begin to change in the light of that comfort. And such light will illuminate the path of connection and lasting joy.

Connecting with Heaven

Heaven is an incredibly powerful source of comfort and strength. But do we really believe it can be? In the difficulty of our suffering, we may need help to have our eyes opened because whether we see it or not, heavenly support *is* there.

Consider the words of Sister Michelle D. Craig of the Young Women General Presidency:

> I love the Old Testament story of a young man who served the prophet Elisha. Early one morning the young man woke up, went outside, and found the city surrounded by a great army intent on destroying them. He ran to Elisha: "Alas, my master! how shall we do?"
>
> Elisha answered, "Fear not: for they that be with us are more than they that be with them."
>
> Elisha knew the young man needed more than calming reassurance; he needed vision. And so "Elisha prayed, . . . Lord, . . . open his eyes, that he may see. And the Lord opened the eyes of

the young man; and he saw: and, behold, the mountain was full of horses and chariots of fire round about Elisha."

There may be times when you, like the servant, find yourself struggling to see how God is working in your life—times when you feel under siege—when the trials of mortality bring you to your knees. Wait and trust in God and in His timing, because you can trust His heart with all of yours.[31]

Letting Him In

In our journey toward healing, we *need* our all-knowing Father to touch our lives, in His perfect way and at His perfect time. That can feel impossible when we're immersed in the darkness of a husband's pornography habit. Although we learn that "the Father is at this moment aware of [us], [our] feelings, and the spiritual and temporal needs of everyone around [us],"[32] such a beautiful truth can sadly be twisted by a pain-stricken mind—"If He is aware, why is He not fixing this? Where is He?"

I have seen questions like "Why is this happening to me?" "Why would God inspire me to marry my husband when He knew about his struggle?" and "Why is He not delivering us from this?" keep heaven's help at arm's length. These thoughts, if stewed over, can keep us from receiving the love and peace Heavenly Father wants to fill us with.

It's common for these and other questions to be a part of the immediate chaos of a betrayal discovery or disclosure. They are fear-based sparks that ignite from feeling spiritually and emotionally unstable. Those sparks can be extinguished when humbly brought to the Father in prayer with faith in Jesus Christ. Or they can grow into a damaging, raging fire within the soul if dwelt on without allowing heaven to intervene.

No matter how we feel about God, the truth is still the truth: The most dependable source of empathy, love, and connection we can

---

31. Michelle D. Craig, "Eyes to See," *Ensign* or *Liahona*, Nov. 2020, 15.
32. Henry B. Eyring, "His Spirit to Be with You," *Ensign* or *Liahona*, May 2018, 88.

access is our Heavenly Father and His Son, Jesus Christ, through the Holy Ghost. They are just *so good* at removing shrapnel.

******

One evening, as I was putting dinner in the oven, the doorbell of our little starter home rang.

It was my son's Primary teacher dropping something off for him. I invited her in and we started talking. Her husband had been imprisoned months prior for sexual crimes as a result of his unchecked sexual behaviors. She was understandably weighed down by the recent discovery of his secret life. Her strength and faith in Jesus Christ were evident as I listened to her tender feelings.

Still, her story stirred within me fears I think most wives of those who give in to sexual escapes have: that those escapes will lead him to do something truly unthinkable. With my unspoken fears in the back of my mind and with tears in my eyes, I told her how inspiring it was that she didn't seem angry with the Lord.

"This went on for so many years without me knowing a thing," she responded. After a pause, and now with tears forming in her own eyes, she continued, "I do wonder at times why I wasn't able to discern well enough as it was going on. Part of me wishes that I would have. But the Lord knew what was happening. And He allowed it to continue. I've come to understand that He has our best interest at heart. I trust that He waited until the right time to bring the truth to light. He waited until I found the Church. He waited until I had been converted to His gospel *enough* that I wouldn't turn away from Him because of the pain I felt. He knows me and knew I would need the perspective and support His gospel gives. It seems like so much suffering could have been avoided if He would have told me sooner. But if He would have, who knows how I would have handled it then. Well, I guess He does, and that's why He waited. He loves me and I can't be angry at that."

The Father and the Son have perfect love for us (see John 17:23; John 15:9; John 3:16), even in our raw and painful emotions and even if we at times feel resentment or anger toward Them. They will never give up on us. They see every aspect and perspective of the trials we are struggling to endure. They even know where every piece of shrapnel is, how big it is, what damage it has done, and what will surface, cleanse, and heal it (see Matthew 6:8). They have a perfect understanding of the evil our marriages are up against and are ever working to bring to pass our coming through it better and sanctified (see Moses 1:39). Even when it doesn't seem like it. Even when our fears and pain tell us Their timing is off or that They've betrayed us. Even when we question or wonder or doubt. The truth still stands: Their plan has already accounted for every injustice we have or will face and provides compensation, opportunity, and redemption for us all. Elder Neal A. Maxwell illustrated this beautifully:

> Real faith in God . . . includes not only faith in Him but faith in His timing; one of the things that is often most difficult for us to have faith in. For instance, God could not rush the restoration, which required, among other things, adequate political and religious freedom. To have rushed would have crushed human agency, or to have risked failure because of prematurity. Instead, God's plan of mercy provided, as we know, for those of the dark ages. And then, the restoration was accomplished on schedule. God's waiting for our readiness continues even now, as History's final events are subject to His redemptiveness. The Lord is not slack concerning His promise as some men count slackness but is longsuffering toward us, not willing that any should perish, but that all should come to repentance (2 Peter 3:9).[33]

When it's put like that, the odds sound pretty stacked up against Satan in this war for the hearts of the children of men. It almost seems foolish of him to keep trying, yet still he moves forward seeking to make all men miserable like unto himself (see 2 Nephi 2:27). He wants to create as much chaos and heartache as he can and take as many casualties down with him along the way—individuals and families alike (see 2 Nephi 2:18).

Looking around at the wickedness of the world and also looking inward at the pain that Satan's influence has caused my family, sometimes it feels more like the odds are stacked against us. In those

---

33. Neal A. Maxwell, "If Thou Endure Well" (Brigham Young University devotional, Dec. 4, 1984), speeches.byu.edu.

moments, I have to remind myself that *we* decide how our marriages will come out at the end of this war. We decide. And we are promised help.

God in His infinite goodness and grace makes Himself *always* available to us (see Doctrine and Covenants 10:5). But He will not force us to receive His influence (see 2 Nephi 2:27; 10:23; Doctrine and Covenants 37:4). Because of the evil that has infiltrated my marriage, there have been times when heaven seemed too far out of reach. "How do I connect with God in this state of darkness?" I would wonder. "How do I reach Someone so good and clean and righteous when I feel so defeated by the adversary?"

The answer? Turn to Him anyway, and don't stop turning to Him until the dawn breaks brightly and the shadows of mortality flee,[34] because with Him, they will. Probably not right away, but there is a loving purpose in that. Elder D. Todd Christofferson taught:

> The process of God-directed purging and purifying will, of necessity, be wrenching and painful at times. Recalling Paul's expression, we are "joint-heirs with Christ; *if so be that we suffer with him, that we may be also glorified together.*"
>
> So, in the midst of this refiner's fire, rather than get angry with God, get close to God. Call upon the Father in the name of the Son. Walk with Them in the Spirit, day by day. Allow Them over time to manifest Their fidelity to you. Come truly to know Them and truly to know yourself. Let God prevail .. . . .
>
> In the end, it is the blessing of a close and abiding relationship with the Father and the Son that we seek. It makes all the difference and is everlastingly worth the cost. We will testify with Paul "that the sufferings of this present [mortal] time are not worthy to be compared with the glory which shall be revealed in us." I bear witness that no matter what our mortal experience may entail, we can trust God and find joy in Him.[35]

---

34. See Jeffrey R. Holland, "Like a Broken Vessel," *Ensign* or *Liahona*, Nov. 2013, 42.
35. D. Todd Christofferson, "Our Relationship with God," *Liahona*, May 2022, 79–80.

God's Opportunity

******

I have very, very difficult pregnancies. Enduring them while also trying to keep it together throughout my husband's repeated pornography viewing was sometimes more than I thought I could handle.

One night during such a time, I felt like I was failing in every aspect of life. I simply did not feel like I was enough. This is an extremely common and overwhelming emotion for many wives after a husband's disclosure of sexual escape. And, at least for me, the "not enough" feeling is always associated with negative self-talk that eats away at the deepest part of my soul.

> Tonight, while trying to fall asleep, negative thoughts and feelings flooded me once again. I was determined, though, to not believe the thoughts and to not let the feelings spiral out of control like they have before, so I tried to combat it all with thoughts like "This isn't real," "That's not true," and "You're a good person."
>
> And then I felt this sweet little baby kick in my belly, and out of desperation to feel some worth, I told myself, "See, Elizabeth, you *are* a good person—look what you're doing and sacrificing to bring her to Earth, even though it's so incredibly hard for you. It's an act of faith, love, and selflessness. See, you *are* good!"
>
> And then, as if Heavenly Father had been standing there all along, watching this conversation unfold in my mind, He made Himself known to me. His presence became so clear and evident. And all at once He wrapped His spiritual arms around me, scooped me up in a warm embrace, and gently corrected me: "Elizabeth, you are good because you are mine." And with those words, every part of me was filled with His love and His thoughts about me, completely replacing the darkness and negativity that had seemed so impenetrable before.
>
> My worth doesn't come from things I do or don't do. It comes from the fact that I'm a daughter of God. And I'm only made aware of that divinity, and changed by it, when I allow myself to truly feel His love. To be moved by His love. To see myself from His perspective.
>
> My soul was so agitated tonight. But once I felt the true love of my Heavenly Father, only then was it able to be completely settled and at peace.

This is the purpose of divine connection. This is the blessing we can obtain when we allow ourselves to suffer *with Him*: He will fill us with His love. If it were up to Him, we would *always* be able to feel that love and the peace and clarity that love brings. We are reminded every Sunday that that is indeed His desire when we hear the words "that they may *always* have His spirit to be with them" (Doctrine and Covenants 20: 77, 79; emphasis added).

Even though it surpasses my understanding, somehow He really is there. Maybe not to remove my suffering instantly or to completely fix my husband or marriage in that exact moment, but He *is* there, ready and wanting to connect with me; to fill me with His love; to help me see things, including myself, clearly; and to remove painful pieces of shrapnel.

And I've learned it's not just Him.

It's Not Just Him

Some years ago, my sister Mae and I decided to take a trip together. We went to visit our parents who were serving a mission in Santiago, Chile. It was a temple mission, which meant they served each day in the temple in Santiago helping members of the Church participate in sacred ordinances and holy worship.

Luke couldn't get work off, so I left him at home and dropped my three young kids off at my in-laws a few hours away. I caught a flight from their house and met Mae (who lived out West) in Florida. From there we would fly together and spend a week with our parents.

Mae and I settled into our seats on the plane in Miami. It was so good to see her—and under such fun circumstances too. We were about to embark on a relaxing, kid-free, Spirit-filled travel adventure! We sat waiting to taxi, talking and laughing and taking selfies. As she turned to her phone to post the picture we had both just approved, I looked down at my phone too. I had a text message from Luke. He relapsed.

It had only been a day. I wasn't even in Chile yet. A flood of sadness, isolation, and frustration washed over me. I tried my best to hide my screen and my reaction so that Mae wouldn't know anything was wrong.

A few days after arriving in Chile, I turned to my journal for an outlet:

> My emotions have been all over the place since learning that Luke relapsed, but I have to hide them this entire trip. I'm really grateful for the time we spend in the temple. Each minute I'm there slowly heals me. I feel connected to and supported by my Heavenly Father, my Savior, and my ancestors. I feel like they're aware of me and my heavy burdens. It's nice to feel like someone here knows what I'm going through, even if they're on the other side of the veil.
>
> I've been doing okay with their help right up until this moment. Right now I feel like I'm about to have a panic attack sparked by shame and depression. And so I guess this process will continue like this, pieces of shrapnel removed by heaven but still more to come up. How many more will surface during this trip? I wish I knew.

At that point, I had been married for many years, so I was relatively good at hiding my emotions in situations where I couldn't isolate myself like I wanted to. And as I flew home after what turned out to be an amazing week, I reflected on the many blessings I received.

I thought visiting Chile would be like my other international trips, experiencing the culture and country and people. But the Lord had other plans for the focus of my visit. I was in the temple most of the time. I performed ordinances every day for hours and the most beautiful thing occurred. The longer I was there, the longer I wanted to stay.

Being someone who has always lived far away from a temple, I usually only ever have time to do one ordinance per temple trip. I've wondered if serving a temple mission or living near a temple where you can be in the temple every day for long periods of time would get monotonous. It wasn't at all! It was like reading the scriptures. The more I opened myself up to the work, the more enlightened and touched by the Spirit I became, and the more I wanted to do.

During my last time in the celestial room in Chile, I felt anxious about going home. I didn't want my trip to end. I worried that the busyness of life would make it hard to have the same connection to heaven I had enjoyed all week. I thought of the people King Benjamin spoke to who wanted "to do good continually" because of the change that had occurred within them from being so filled with the Holy Ghost (Mosiah 5:2). I also thought about the people Jesus Christ visited in the Americas after His Resurrection. They pleaded with Him to stay a little longer because they didn't want such a sacred, beautiful experience with divinity to end (see 3 Nephi 17). There I sat in the holiest of places feeling the same way.

I felt like no matter what was going on in my marriage, if I was in the temple, I would feel and hear from God. I yearned to never leave the safety or clarity within those walls. I was filled with love and peace. I was gaining perspective. My brief moment in mortality and the pain that often consumed me was being "[projected] onto the wide screen of eternity."[36]

I was also receiving personal revelation at a rate and in such a powerful way that I never had before. It was like when I realized as a youth the benefit of praying longer than five minutes—you know, longer than your normal nighttime personal prayer that you quickly mutter before crashing onto the pillow. I discovered that if I intentionally spent actual time with the Lord in prayer, the longer I prayed, the closer I would feel to Him and the more He was able to do with my often confused and troubled heart. That's what happened in the temple. I spent longer than my normal "five minutes" there and it unlocked a world of peace, direction, and healing. I wanted everyone to experience it, especially Luke.

On the plane ride home, I thought back to when we started planning the trip. I was on the phone with my parents and mentioned how I would love to come visit them. I saw then how the Spirit took control of our conversation and guided me, my parents, and my in-laws in making it happen so I could have the experiences I had within the house of the Lord in such a unique way. I will always be grateful to them for that.

I did wonder, though, why the Lord would guide me there for that week knowing Luke would have such a hard time while I was gone. He was so lonely, depressed, and discouraged. He relapsed several times. God had to know he would struggle.

---

36. Neil L. Andersen, "Wounded," *Ensign* or *Liahona*, Nov. 2018, 85.

Prior to my trip, it felt like we had been at a standstill with his recovery, not knowing what to do next. He didn't really relapse at that time of our lives unless we were apart and he was alone. And when he did relapse, it was usually the same old thing: I went through my difficult emotions alone, he went through his, and we both just tried to move forward. Then time made the pain slightly fade until he relapsed again. It was a cycle we didn't know how to break. He seemed to have such a repentant and soft heart at that point. We didn't understand why he still struggled so much. But after my week in Chile, things became much more clear for us both.

******

The first night I was back home, and Luke and I could really talk after the kids were asleep, we sat on our bed, held hands, and took a deep breath. It was strange because we were both smiling—not the usual way we started off a discussion about his relapses.

"Okay, you first," I said, beaming. "Why are you smiling?"

"I know I had a really hard time while you were gone, which we already talked a little about on the phone once you got back to the States, but the other night I had the most amazing spiritual experience," Luke said. He told me about his week, the difficulties he had, and how he tried so hard to access God's help. "He did help," he explained. "He touched my heart and taught me—*really* taught me." He shared the details of a revelation he received while studying Doctrine and Covenants 123, particularly while reading the chapter's closing encouragement: "Therefore, dearly beloved brethren, let us cheerfully do all things that lie in our power; and then may we stand still, with the utmost assurance, to see the salvation of God, and for his arm to be revealed" (verse 17).

Luke was so broken while I was gone, but he turned to the Lord who responded with the empathy, connection, and direction he needed. It was beautiful to hear the details of his sacred experience.

We cried. We hugged. Then he asked, "So why were you smiling?"

I told him about my week and how it ended up being a week of revelation for me as well. I told him that since learning of his relapse while on the plane and fearing he would continue to relapse all week,

I went to the temple completely desperate for comfort. Every time I was there, I would feel a piece of what I needed given to me by the Lord. I knew more would come if I just allowed myself to receive it. And that's exactly what happened. The Savior helped me to see my marriage and Luke through His eyes. He taught me things about Luke that I hadn't known or internalized before. He also showed me what I can do to help heal our marriage. Every day my heart softened a little more because of the communication I received from the Lord in the temple.

I also felt buoyed up by my ancestors. I learned that they care *deeply* for us. They counsel about us and about how to be involved in our lives to provide us with tender mercies that our Heavenly Father wants us to have (see 1 Nephi 1:20). I shared with Luke the incredible way my week of revelation began.

After landing in Chile, we put our bags down, ate, and headed straight to the temple before it closed for the night. I sat on a couch facing the baptismal font and waited while Mae was baptized for many of our ancestors. I would be up next with another large batch of family names, but all that filled my mind was the fact that Luke had told me about his relapse just hours prior and that it would probably be the first of many throughout the week. I sat there feeling very burdened and sad.

All of a sudden, my spiritual eyes were opened and I saw countless spirits standing everywhere. The room was full! They all looked toward the font with peace and excitement. I knew in my heart and mind that they were the ancestors being baptized as well as many of their loved ones. It brought me joy to be there with them. But as I looked around, I started to feel ashamed. I was so focused on the trials of my life during their special moment. Disappointed with my selfishness, I looked down at my lap and began to cry.

Then, I felt my great-great-great-grandmother, whose name is also Elizabeth, sitting next to me and her mother sitting next to her. One of the ancestors I was going to be baptized for was her grandmother. I had spent many years working to find Elizabeth and her family. Her presence was very familiar, and I felt her spiritual arm fall around my shoulders as we sat there together.

She knew. She knew it all. Spirit to spirit, she told me to not feel ashamed that I brought such a burdened heart to the temple. "There isn't a better place to bring such a heart!" She taught me that she and my other ancestors know the trials faced by me and my little family. They find such joy and purpose in helping us through them. Still with her arm around me, she smiled as she gave me a tender side squeeze. "It will be alright," she reassured me. "We are aware of you and are with you more often than you realize." I felt so close to her and to all my ancestors.

When it was my turn, I got into the warm water and stood next to my dad. He held my arms to begin the baptisms. His grip was strong and secure. I looked up into his face and felt bonded with him. I looked around the room and saw my mom and my sister. I was filled with their unconditional love for me. Being with them was more supportive, helpful, and healing than I had anticipated. Even though they didn't know my turmoil, our spirits were connected and I thought my heart would burst.

Then I looked around at all the spirits that were still opened to my view. I felt that so many were not only accepting the work I was doing for them but were grateful I would come and do it even with such a broken heart. They were touched that I would look beyond my own pain and still act as a type of savior to help them progress on the covenant path.

I was worried that my sorrow would ruin their special moment, but the opposite was true. The strength I had to do their work, instead of locking myself in my room and hiding under the covers, showed my love for them and for Jesus Christ's great cause.

Luke and I finished a beautiful night of conversation and connection about our week. We cuddled, basking in the warm light of personal revelation.

******

A few days later, I was in the kitchen listening to soothing hymns while putting the dishes away. Luke was outside playing with the kids. As I reached up to put a plastic toddler bowl into the cupboard, my heart became filled with warmth and peace. I put the bowl down, looked over my left shoulder, and felt another sacred presence. I couldn't see her and didn't know who she was, but I could feel where she was in the room and that she knew and loved me. Her message was brief yet powerful. Spirit to spirit, she acknowledged the concerns I had the last time I was in the celestial room in Chile. Then she tenderly reassured me, "We're still with you. The veil is as thin or as thick as you make it."

When the experience ended, I wiped a tear with one hand and steadied myself against the counter with the other. My mind turned to a testimony by President Jeffrey R. Holland that I love dearly:

> From the beginning down through the dispensations, God has used angels as His emissaries in conveying love and concern for His children. . . . Usually such beings are *not* seen. Sometimes they are. But seen or unseen they are *always* near. Sometimes their assignments are very grand and have significance for the whole world. Sometimes the messages are more private. Occasionally the angelic purpose is to warn. But most often it is to comfort, to provide some form of merciful attention, guidance in difficult times.[37]

I have "[beheld] angels and ministering spirits" (Moroni 10:14) and have had many encounters with those on the other side of the veil. So when I say connect with heaven, I literally mean *connect with heaven*. There are more opportunities to do so in this war for the hearts of the children of men than most of us realize, because truly, "they that be with us *are* more than they that be with them" (2 Kings 6:16; emphasis added). Remember, a prophet of God has promised that "every time you worthily serve and worship in the temple, you leave armed with God's power and with His angels having 'charge over' you."[38]

"Therefore, dearly beloved brethren, let us cheerfully do all things that lie in our power; and then may we stand still, with the utmost assurance, to see the salvation of God, *and for his arm to be revealed*" (Doctrine and Covenants 123:17; emphasis added).

---

37. Jeffrey R. Holland, "The Ministry of Angels," *Ensign* or *Liahona*, Nov. 2008, 29.
38. Russell M. Nelson, "Spiritual Treasures," *Ensign* or *Liahona*, Nov. 2019, 78.

Part 3:
I Can

I can be enabled and strengthened by Jesus Christ to act in my circumstances instead of being acted upon by them.

Some of the things I can feel empowered to do:

I can let my spouse take responsibility.
I can love my spouse as Jesus Christ loves us.
I can face this evil with my spouse.
I can see my husband through God's eyes.
I can keep my covenants.
I can experience true intimacy.
I can help others.
I can be humble.
I can come to be grateful for this extremity.

12
I can let my spouse take responsibility

SOMETIMES I AM MY OWN WORST ENEMY. I USED TO THINK THAT IF *I* was somehow different, Luke wouldn't view pornography. I tried in vain to take upon myself what we thought was a sexual addiction. I mistakenly assumed I was the cause and therefore also believed that I needed to be the solution. I dwelled on this idea for three reasons.

One, I honestly wanted to help Luke. I love him. His happiness is one of my highest priorities. And when he gives into temptation of any kind, he isn't happy.

Two, I didn't want to feel pain anymore. Every time Luke turned to pornography, my oxygen was yanked away from me all over again. The disconnection it created was unbearable.

Three, I felt like I needed to do something about the trajectory of our family. The eternal nature of it seemed to be slipping through my fingers. So I tried to change what I could: myself. Here are some of the ways I did this throughout the years:

- Paying extreme attention to how I looked, hoping to be attractive "enough" so he would turn to me instead of pornography.
- Not being myself—mimicking the world's way of intimacy, hoping to be sexy "enough" to compete with what Luke was viewing and pull his attention back to our marriage.
- Never saying no and being hypersexual so I could please him "enough," hoping his needs would be met and that he wouldn't look elsewhere.
- Being overbearing—treating him like I was the mother and he was the child to be helpful "enough" to keep him on track with his efforts to stop viewing pornography (scheduling therapy sessions for him, constantly reminding him of appointments or tasks he was supposed to be doing as recovery homework, asking the dreaded question, keeping my true feelings to myself so I didn't cause him pain, etc.).
- Being intentionally passive-aggressive or mean, or detaching from him more than I wanted to, hoping that if I punished him "enough," he'd feel so bad about our situation that he would stop.

Spoiler alert: none of these were helpful. In fact, they were extremely toxic lies and behaviors that hurt us individually and damaged our marriage as a whole. Why? This is a great example of one of Satan's most powerful tactics he uses to bind us as his: perversion. He takes a truth and distorts it to become a philosophy of man mingled with scripture (see Acts 20:30; Moroni 7:17; 1 John 2:22).

- The scripture part of this example: We can be "empowered through the Atonement to *act* as agents (see Doctrine and Covenants 58:26–29) and *impact* [our] circumstances."[39]
- Satan's perversion: If I change things about myself, I can *get Luke* to behave righteously.

But Satan's perversions will always leave us comfortless. This warning by Joseph F. Smith says it all:

---

39. David A. Bednar, "Bear Up Their Burdens with Ease," *Ensign* or *Liahona*, May 2014, 89.

Let it not be forgotten that the evil one has great power in the earth and that by every possible means he seeks to darken the minds of men and then offers them falsehood and deception in the guise of truth. Satan is a skillful imitator, and as genuine gospel truth is given the world in ever-increasing abundance, so he spreads the counterfeit coin of false doctrine. Beware of his spurious currency, it will purchase for you nothing but disappointment, misery and spiritual death. The "father of lies" he has been called, and such an adept has he become, through the ages of practice in his nefarious work, that were it possible he would deceive the very elect.[40]

In this deception, I was breathing in carbon monoxide instead of the oxygen I needed. It seemed to make sense at the time because at least I was breathing in *something* that felt a little like the air of safety, stability, and attachment. I had good intentions. I wanted to help. I wanted us both to heal and be happy. But because this issue wasn't really about me or about sex—because I based my efforts on a perversion instead of an eternal truth, and because I'm not the One who performed the atoning sacrifice meant to empower Luke to use his agency righteously[41]—I was still left gasping for air.

Through prayerful reflection, the Lord taught me this unaltered truth: I am not the cause of this pornography problem, nor am I the solution. There *are* things I can control and change about myself to help heal our marriage, which I have talked about in this book and will talk more about in the coming chapters. But that is vastly different than changing and controlling myself *in order to* change and control *Luke*.

The goal of my personal improvement is to draw closer to Jesus Christ, who is "the way, the truth, and the life" (John 14:6); to invite the Holy Ghost into our home; and to be guided to know "when to speak, what to say, and yes, on some occasions, when to be still. Remember, our [husbands] already chose to follow the Savior in their premortal realm. Sometimes it is only by their own life's experiences

---

40. Joseph F. Smith, in Daniel H. Ludlow, ed., *Latter-day Prophets Speak* (Bookcraft, 1948), 20–21.
41. See Isaiah 53:6; Acts 13:38; 2 Corinthians 5:18; Mosiah 13:28; Helaman 5:9; Moroni 10:33.

that those sacred feelings are awakened again. Ultimately, the choice to love and follow the Lord has to be their own."[42]

And so it's not healthy, helpful, or right to try to take the burden of Luke's choices on myself. I don't have the capacity to. It simply isn't my role. Instead, as his wife, I'm in a great position to *love him* as he works with the Deliverer through the maze of deliverance.

******

Church yesterday was a really, really hard day. It was fast and testimony meeting and the first Sunday with our new bishopric. Almost all the testimonies were about the new bishopric and how amazing they are, how prepared they are, and how called of God they are. I'm not going to lie, it was painful. Not because I don't think that of our new bishopric. I do—they are absolutely wonderful men who will do a fantastic job. But it was just a reminder to me of the confusion I feel around Luke's interview and having that call extended to him then *not* extended to him.

After having a week to process my feelings, I've come to realize that my confusion and pain have to do with two possibilities. Either, one, Luke wasn't in a place spiritually to accept the Lord's call. Or, two, Luke was in a place spiritually to accept His call, and the stake president was clouded by his frustration with Luke and mistaken in his decision.

The first possibility hurts because Luke is my husband, the patriarch of our home, and I want him to always be able to do what the Lord asks. I want that of myself too. It's not about what the specific call from the Lord ever is—this call could have been anything. It's that he apparently wasn't ready and worthy to do what the Lord asked. This first possibility is confusing because I thought Luke was in a good place spiritually, and it actually had been a long time since he relapsed before the interview. He has such a tender, beautiful heart. He is so repentant and humble. He loves the Lord. He wants to do his very best for Him and for us. This possibility makes the traumatized side of me worry that I don't know Luke as well as I thought, or maybe the Lord knows something

---

42. Robert D. Hales, "'Come, Follow Me' by Practicing Christian Love and Service," *Ensign* or *Liahona*, Nov. 2016, 24.

I don't about his progress or lack thereof. Or maybe it's that I don't understand what the Lord is looking for because I really thought Luke had it.

The second option is painful because I don't want Luke to miss out on this wonderful opportunity to serve the Lord in this way and all the blessings that would come to him from doing so. After his interview, he lay on our bed with his head in my lap and just cried. One of the things he said was how he feels like he has missed such a great learning opportunity because, as he put it, "What better people to serve with in my first bishopric than Bishop Stewart and Brother Smith?" They are very similar to Luke in their temperament, and he really loves both of them. I knew his comment had reference to a future call that has always made him feel nervous. His patriarchal blessing says he will serve as a bishop at some point, but he has never felt confident in himself enough to feel comfortable with that. I think he realizes that he could have learned so much from Bishop Stewart and Brother Smith, which could have helped prepare him for a future call that is already overwhelming him. In his crying, it was clear that he doesn't want to let the Lord down.

It breaks my heart to think Luke might really be worthy and ready for that call and that he's missing it because a leader has possibly misunderstood him. And not just how this bishopric calling would be good for Luke, but I also keep thinking of all the people he could help in this leadership position. He is prayerful, meek, empathetic, and the best communicator I know. But I know the Lord's work cannot be frustrated, and I know He compensates for how the mistakes of others negatively affect our lives. I know these things. But it still hurts.

All during church I kept wondering, Which is it? The first possibility or the second? I can't get this out of my head. All day and all night and all morning, I've wondered. I don't know how I'll move on from this. I desperately want to spend time in the temple. I wish I could. I wish it wasn't so far, and I wish I didn't have to feel rushed or guilty because someone would be watching the kids for so long. I feel trapped in my own mind, in my own confusion, in my own pain. This morning I woke up and just wanted to ignore the world and stay in bed all day.

> Whether it's the first or the second possibility, my fear has been triggered in a very intense way. I keep picturing a scene of the early Saints about to head out west. There everyone is gathered together, handcarts assembled, provisions secured. And there we are, Luke and I and our little family, standing excitedly among the crowd. But then, even though we want to be with God's people—go where they go, do what they do—we are left behind, told to stay because we are not prepared "enough." All because of Luke looking at pornography. How many more ways can this affliction bring our family heartache? How many more blessings will it rob us of? How many more tears will we shed because of it? Will it be the thing that keeps us from being with the Lord in the end?
>
> A part of me knows that these fears are just based on lies from the adversary. This is his scare tactic to put a wedge between not only me and Luke but between us and the Lord and His Church. I can't let that happen.
>
> Wow—I just realized that I actually have come a long way. That thought, "I can't let that happen," would have meant something very different years ago. It would have meant that I was going to make some random, huge change in myself to try to change and control Luke. But I've learned through painful experience and by the grace of God that that approach is spiritually destructive. Now, "I can't let that happen" means I recognize a fear I'm having, I see how it's made me vulnerable to Satan's lies, and I determine that I won't fall for the trap, even when I feel like I'm not wanted—not wanted by Luke, by the Lord, or by His people. How do I combat the lies? With the truth.

After that journal entry, I went to the scriptures for comfort. They always do a good job of shining light on the truth. In my prayerful search, the Spirit brought me to Doctrine and Covenants 27. I read the chapter and wasn't really getting anything until the last verse, which ends with the words "be faithful until I come, and ye shall be caught up, that *where I am ye shall be also.* Amen" (verse 18; emphasis added).

When I read those words, they flowed through my mind with great power as if in the voice of Jesus Christ Himself. This is a specific desire of His and a literal invitation to us. I knew in that moment, with a surety I didn't have before, that I am a daughter of God and that there is nowhere He would rather I be than *with Him*. He loves me and He loves Luke. With this reassurance also came guidance. The Spirit impressed upon me that the best way I can help our family "be faithful until [He] comes" is to simply love—love the Lord and love Luke. I felt strengthened, once and for all, to forever leave behind Satan's perversions and my desire to control others.

Love him. That is my place in all of this. And it's so important that it gets its own chapter.

13
I can love my spouse as Jesus Christ loves us

"Okay, so I get that my role is to love my husband, but that's what I thought I was doing by always checking up on him and trying to prevent a relapse," I used to tell myself. "I mean, if Luke was about to walk in front of a semitruck, wouldn't I call out a warning to him at the very least? I'm not going to just let him walk into a bad situation!"

Yes, but the way I was trying to show love to Luke was not allowing him to take responsibility for his actions. Realizing this made me think about our perfect example of love: Jesus Christ. He loves us and then invites us to love others in the same way. "A new commandment I give unto you, that ye love one another; *as I have loved you*, that ye also love one another" (John 13:34; emphasis added).

So how does He love us? He uses boundaries, serves us, and bonds with us through the Holy Ghost.

Jesus Christ Uses Boundaries

Simply put, a boundary establishes what is and isn't okay within a relationship—what is and isn't expected and wanted. It is meant to encourage growth, trust, and connection while protecting us and our relationship from physical, spiritual, and emotional harm. Jesus Christ lovingly uses boundaries with us. In order to access His strengthening and redemptive powers, as well as His peace, He gives us commandments to obey and requires repentance when we don't (see Mormon 3:2; 3 Nephi 18:25, 32).

We can also hold our own boundaries, especially around our partners' efforts toward recovery. But to be honest, making and keeping boundaries was always a really difficult concept for me to understand and live. It sounded a lot like trying to control Luke's recovery efforts through ultimatums. That's exactly what boundaries can become if that's the intention behind them. It's all in the intention.

A revelation given to the prophet Joseph Smith sheds light on what the Lord's intention is behind the boundaries He sets:

> 10 Remember the worth of souls is great in the sight of God;
>
> 11 For, behold, the Lord your Redeemer suffered death in the flesh; wherefore he suffered the pain of all men [the boundary He kept], that all men might repent and come unto him [the boundary we are asked to keep].
>
> 12 And he hath risen again from the dead, *that he might bring all men unto him,* on conditions of repentance.
>
> 13 And how great is his *joy* in the soul that repenteth! (Doctrine and Covenants 18:10–13; emphasis added)

These verses lay out His responsibility in the relationship, our responsibility, and the result of both staying true to those responsibilities: connection and joy! He doesn't give us commandments and require repentance to control us. He does it to "bring all men unto him," or in other words, to form and strengthen an attachment bond with us. He wants to connect! That means each commandment is intentionally given to create the best environment for us to bond with divinity.

From this we learn the purpose behind keeping effective boundaries in our marriages. It is to create and nurture a healthy attachment with our spouse. To keep the integrity of that purpose intact, when we make our boundaries, we need to be careful that we are not making them out of anger, frustration, resentment, or manipulation.

The years that were most damaging for Luke and me were the ones in which we didn't make or hold healthy boundaries. I did this for different reasons at different times. Sometimes it was because I thought I was helping him by not making him feel bad that I was hurt. Other times I was in denial and ignored that I felt emotionally unstable and betrayed. I was exhausted by our situation and didn't know what to do, so I did nothing.

Whatever the reason, I was being acted upon by my circumstances. Using boundaries appropriately allows me to act. It helps me say, "Our marriage is meant to be an environment for us to get the attachment we both need. So what actions can we take and what boundaries can we set in order to create that environment?"

Our relationship used to be a garden that brought forth blossoms of love, joy, selflessness, and beauty. But because of the effects of lust, our garden began dying, and in it, *so were we*. We needed to be in an environment that would facilitate healing and growth, like a greenhouse. Within its walls, our marriage could begin to flourish again. And in it, *so could we*.

Still in use today, our boundaries are the things we both decide we need to do to keep our marriage in our greenhouse. They give us the place, time, and resources that consistent growth and progress call for. They allow us to act together against what feels like a constant flow of threats to our bond, like pornography, instead of being acted upon and damaged by them.

What will help repair your greenhouse and keep your marriage within the safety of its walls? Maybe you both go to therapy consistently. Maybe you start praying together on a daily basis, attend the temple together regularly, or both. Maybe you journal when you feel a piece of shrapnel surfacing. Maybe he reaches out to people in his support group when he's feeling triggered to escape. You could exercise together a couple of evenings a week. Or perhaps you both review your day with the Feelings Wheel each night. Maybe you won't ask the dreaded question and he'll tell you within a certain amount of time if he relapses. The options are endless.

Which boundaries to make and focus on will be specific to each situation and relationship. The key to finding out what that looks like for you is to establish boundaries at a time "when moved upon by the Holy Ghost" (Doctrine and Covenants 121:43). Discuss them together. Make them official. Make them a priority. Most importantly, make them prayerfully.

The Holy Ghost can help us to "know the truth of *all* things" (Moroni 10:5; emphasis added). *All things* includes which boundaries will be most effective within each marriage—that is, which boundaries will allow the afflicted to feel the natural consequences of their actions while at the same time promoting healing and stability for the individual, family, and marriage.

I looked through so many books and blogs and articles hoping that one of them would tell me word for word what boundaries to make. The problem was that none of those resources knew me, Luke, or our situation specifically. By working with the Holy Ghost and our therapist, who did know us and was also trying to be prayerful in his efforts to help, we were able to make boundaries that reestablished a greenhouse-type environment. It was a slow rebuild. I didn't realize it then, but loving as Christ loves by using boundaries allowed us the time we needed to heal without our marriage burning in the meantime from flames of recurrent explosions.

******

Even when we know boundaries are important, enforcing them can still feel very daunting. But remember, we can always look to our heavenly parents and our Savior—our perfect examples—to see how they set boundaries with us and how they encourage us to keep those boundaries. If we look and listen, they will show us how to do it *their* way—a way that is driven by love; a way that is free from shame, resentment, manipulation, and unrighteous dominion; a way that empowers, inspires, and connects.

One Sunday morning, I reluctantly opened my eyes to the sound of a toddler crying. Without sitting up, I looked around my room. The sun was barely beginning to peek through the shades, so I knew my sleepless night was almost over. I had been woken up several times throughout the night by different kids for different reasons, which, tragically, was becoming a nightly tradition. It left me exhausted in every way. I had a very demanding calling at the time, and I figured the rest I needed that day would definitely not be found at church.

"I need sleep," I rationalized as I came back to my bed after comforting our youngest. Feeling overwhelmed with my life and lack of physical and emotional energy, I started forming a plan for who I could ask to take over my church responsibilities for the day. When I decided who to text, the tiniest twinge of something pricked my heart. I tried to ignore it. I *really* didn't want to go, but I thought that perhaps I'd give it a few minutes before asking anyone.

Lying down now, I closed my eyes. But instead of sleep, my mind turned to my heavenly parents and Savior. I saw their brilliant faces (how I picture them anyway). They were standing together in front of me, and I could feel the love flowing from them. Their eyes were soft and their smiles gentle. Moved by their incredible love for me, the thought came that I wanted to be someone they could depend on and trust. So I pulled myself out of bed. I knew where they wanted me to be.

Trying to get ourselves and a bunch of kids ready for church created a very busy morning for me and Luke. By the time we all shuffled into our cultural hall row of chairs, I was completely spent. I handed out the snacks and the coloring books and all the things that should help the hour go smoothly for our kids (but for some reason never do), then grabbed the hymnbook for the opening song. I flipped to the page while humming along with the organ playing the introduction.

"Oh, I love this song," I thought to myself and then began singing the first verse with the congregation, not realizing the message that was waiting for me in the lyrics:

> It may not be on the mountain height
> Or over the stormy sea,
> It may not be at the battle's front
> My Lord will have need of me.

Then, I remembered my early morning dilemma and decision.

> But if, by a still, small voice he calls
> To paths that I do not know,
> I'll answer, dear Lord, with my hand in thine:
> I'll go where you want me to go.

The Spirit warmed every part of me and put these words into my mind: "Thank you for coming. You were right—this is where we want you to be because today this is where we are. Elizabeth, you *are* someone we can depend on." With tears in my eyes and a renewed energy I didn't think I was capable of having that day, I *resolutely* sang the chorus as my reply in this divine conversation:

> I'll go where you want me to go, dear Lord,
> Over mountain or plain or sea;
> I'll say what you want me to say, dear Lord;
> I'll be what you want me to be.[43]

I sang the rest of the song, incredibly grateful to have made covenants with God in which I promised to keep the commandments. Those covenants established the loving expectations of my heavenly parents and *brought me to them* where I could have such a sacred encounter. I was also grateful for how kindly they reminded me of those expectations that morning, and I realized that when done in this way, *their* way, boundaries can be a beautiful, wonderful, tender blessing that stabilizes the relationship and brings great joy.

Jesus Christ Serves Us

Another way Jesus Christ shows His love for us is through service. During His mortal ministry He said, "I am among you as he that serveth" (Luke 22:27). In our quest to love our spouse, we can look

---

43. "I'll Go Where You Want Me to Go," *Hymns*, no. 270.

to Christ's example of how to serve through prayer, by lightening the load of others, and by allowing others to serve us.

Serving My Spouse through Prayer

After explaining He was on Earth to serve, Jesus Christ elaborated on one of the ways He fulfilled that purpose.

"Simon, Simon," He said, "behold, Satan hath desired to have you, that he may sift you as wheat: *But I have prayed for thee*, that thy faith fail not: and when thou art converted, strengthen thy brethren" (Luke 22:31–32; emphasis added).

I often feel that Satan desires to have my husband and that I'm powerless against him. But then I remember there is great power in prayer to combat him (see Doctrine and Covenants 10:5) and obtain "the highest of all blessings," even "to secure for ourselves *and for others* blessings that God is already willing to grant but that are made conditional on our asking for them" (Bible Dictionary, "Prayer"; emphasis added).

The most beautiful example of Jesus Christ praying for each of us is when He was in the Garden of Gethsemane. As wives, it's comforting to remember that He prayed over the very struggles and sins that are damaging the healthy attachment bond within our marriages. During that sacred time, He felt all that we have felt, feel now, and ever will feel concerning our spouse's choices (see Alma 7:11–12). He knows what it feels like when we have our oxygen taken away. He felt every blow, every explosion, every piece of shrapnel that has forced its way into our flesh. He also felt all that our spouse feels, even the very urges that drive his pull toward lustful escapes.

Not only does our husbands' attachment to pornography try to compete for priority in our relationships, but it also creates a secondary, counterfeit, competing attachment in his relationship with the Savior. How did Christ respond to this form of rejection when He felt it in the Garden of Gethsemane? He prayed to the Father for understanding and strength. Then He pressed on until His service to our husbands, His atoning sacrifice, was complete despite the exquisite pain it caused Him (see Doctrine and Covenants 19:16–19). Jesus Christ didn't ignore that pain, nor did He let it make Him resentful toward our husbands or cause Him to give up on them. Instead, He laid it at the feet of a loving, ever-present Heavenly Father in prayer (see Luke 22:41–42), just as we can.

How did Heavenly Father respond to Jesus Christ's submissiveness? He sent an angel to be with Him, and from that, Christ was strengthened to be able to serve our husbands the best way He could (see Luke 22:43–44). When we rely on Heavenly Father as He did, we too can be strengthened to serve and love our husbands the best way we can.

******

My efforts to pray for Luke began as short, angry prayers. I would express all the betrayal I felt as well as my disgust and frustration about our situation. My heart was hardened from the lack of oxygen it had endured. It was scarred from so many pieces of shrapnel buried within it. Rather than praying for my husband, as Christ did for Simon, I really was just praying out of desperation for someone, *anyone*, to not only understand what I was going through but to go through it with me.

Over time I realized that my one-sided conversations with Heavenly Father weren't as beneficial as they could have been. I needed to give Him the opportunity to speak. Little by little I would quiet my mouth and mind as I prayed—mostly toward the end when I was done getting out all that I needed to say. In one prayer, I would give Him maybe five seconds of a humble ear. In the next prayer, I would try my best to stretch it to ten. This pattern continued until finally my heart was soft enough to actually want to have Him reply instead of just listen to my heartbreak. And He did.

The many prayers that once were filled with anger and confusion evolved into sacred, tender experiences of direction and peace. They truly became "living discussions with [my] Heavenly Father."[44] Often I would start a prayer and not say a word so that He could speak first. I would listen with an open heart, knowing and trusting He was there to sit with me in my pain and strengthen me to press on. I realized

---

44. Russell M. Nelson, "Think Celestial!," *Liahona*, Nov. 2023, 118.

His was an attachment bond I could rely on one hundred percent of the time.

Just as I had heard in the audiobook "Strengthening Recovery Through Strengthening Marriage" (see chapter 3),[45] I came to better understand that Heavenly Father is my perfect parent and I am His child. Because of that, He will always be accessible and responsive to my feelings in the way that is best for me. "As soon as we learn the true relationship in which we stand toward God (namely, God is our Father, and we are His children), then at once prayer becomes natural and instinctive on our part. Many of the so-called difficulties about prayer arise from forgetting this relationship" (Bible Dictionary, "Prayer").

Once my prayers changed in this way, I felt capable of praying for Luke. I was getting attention, attachment, and oxygen from my Heavenly Father, made possible through the Atonement of Jesus Christ and delivered to me by way of the Holy Ghost. They were consistently helping me remove shrapnel. I felt heard and loved, so my loneliness started to diminish. Their accessibility and responsiveness became like an angel sent to strengthen me (not to mention the actual angels sent to strengthen me). With this source of comfort, I could now think of and plead for my husband's deliverance from the adversary with the right intentions, hoping, as Christ hoped for Simon, that his faith wouldn't fail him (see Luke 22:32).

Serving My Spouse by Lightening His Load

Once my prayers and pleadings were humble, the Lord bestowed upon me a portion of His love for Luke (see Moroni 7:48). This helped me want to serve him every day. I wanted to keep the house clean and do his laundry so he wouldn't have to worry about it. I wanted to rub his head and neck and back because I knew he would appreciate it. I wanted to give him genuine compliments so he would know I thought about him. I wanted to really listen when he talked to me so I wouldn't miss anything he had to say. His words and feelings became

---

45. Kevin B. Skinner and Geoff Steurer, "Strengthening Recovery Through Strengthening Marriage" (K. Skinner Corp., 2015), audio CD.

important to me again. I wanted to understand and empathize with him, even when his feelings were difficult for me to hear.

The Lord also helped me see the things Luke had been doing to draw closer to Him. With that came a deep appreciation for the humility in Luke that I was blinded to for so long because of my own pain. And in the times Luke wasn't so humble and Satan had a strong hold of his heart, seeing him through God's eyes carried me through. It helped me to continue to serve him out of pure, authentic, Christlike love.

It was remarkable. *My* heart was changing (see Mosiah 5:2). It was becoming more like my Savior's. My service to Luke is nowhere near as significant as how Jesus Christ served him in the Garden of Gethsemane or how He continues to serve Luke now on a daily basis. But this is the way that *I can* serve Luke. It isn't easy and I'm not perfect at it, even after years of practice. But this is how I can try to love him as the Savior loves him, even when his choices cause me pain.

It's easy to forget what the Savior did for *me* in the Garden of Gethsemane. It wasn't only my husband He was praying for in those sacred moments of agony. "Behold, [Elizabeth]," I can hear in my mind, "Satan hath desired to have you [by keeping your heart hard and unable to serve and love your husband because of the pain he has caused you], that he may sift you as wheat: But I have prayed for thee, that thy faith fail not: and when thou art converted [or filled with the Savior's love], strengthen thy brethren [even he that caused you pain]" (Luke 22:31–32).

Accepting Service from My Spouse

Having love and harmony flow between two wounded spouses is not only about serving the afflicted but also accepting the service he tries to give as well. There were times when my pain and desire to push Luke away kept me from receiving the things he was doing to try to rebuild connection. But when I did let his kindness in, it became a source of unexpected comfort.

One night I was having an especially hard time and was trying to distract myself by watching television. Luke came into the room and asked me to go into the bathroom alone. Annoyed but somewhat curious, I went. He had drawn me a warm bath, placed a copy of the most recent *Ensign* magazine on the edge of the tub next to a large glass of ice water, and lined the rest of the edge with lit candles.

"He knows me so well," I thought to myself with a little smile. That thought was quickly followed by a much harsher one: "Yeah, he knows me so well—and yet he still hurts me."

Even in my anger, I couldn't resist my favorite way to relax, so I got into the warm, bubbly water. When I did, I noticed he had taped a picture of Jesus Christ to the wall next to the bath faucet so I could see it as I soaked. It was a picture of Him coming out of His tomb with an arm outstretched, as if He was looking directly at the painter as He emerged. My pain gave me a deeper twinge of frustration that Luke would try to do something so nice for me when he was the cause of my heartache. But as I lay there looking into the eyes of my Savior, I was overcome with the Spirit and my anger began to melt away.

With the picture positioned as it was, I felt as though Jesus Christ was coming out of His tomb right in front of me. In my mind, I ran up to Him in that beautiful garden and buried my face in His chest. I could feel the linen fabric of His ivory robe rub against my tear-stained face as His open arms wrapped around me. I took a long, deep breath in. My nose filled with a clay-like, earthy scent. It was calming. His strong embrace was stable and secure. I didn't want that moment to end. I was known and loved.

It felt so real. I was being held by the Lamb of God. His very attentive presence reassured me that the comfort I was enjoying didn't have to end when my mind brought me out of the picture and back to my bath. His love and empathy is always available to me.

For the rest of my bath, I was left to ponder on Luke's thoughtfulness. He too wanted to follow Christ's instruction to Simon to "strengthen [his] brethren" (Luke 22:32). For Luke, that meant me.

While soaking in the tub, I finally saw the beauty and healing that could occur if I stopped putting up walls around my wounded soul and accepted the heartfelt efforts of a broken husband just trying his best.

Jesus Christ Bonds with Us through the Holy Ghost

Once my heart began to soften and was strengthened by the healthy attachment bond I was developing again with the Godhead, I was in a better place emotionally to reach out to Luke for attachment as well. So I looked to Jesus Christ's example of how to form a healthy bond.

The Savior wants us to get to know Him through experiences we have with the Holy Ghost. One of the Holy Ghost's main roles is to confirm to us that what we're learning about Jesus Christ is true. Thus, we come to see, know, love, and appreciate Him in a way that cannot be mimicked, altered, perverted, or overshadowed by the adversary (see John 14:16–19). And so it is with our spouses. When we have experiences together with our husbands *and* the Holy Ghost, the Holy Ghost will help us to see, know, love, and appreciate them in the eternal light of truth. As it is with the Savior, this approach to getting to know each other cannot be mimicked, altered, perverted, or overshadowed by the adversary.

Of course, we can neglect or minimize those experiences to the point that they do not bond us to our spouses, or to the Savior for that matter. But if we are intentional about this divine way of getting to know someone, then we will be on the very path to bond with our husbands that the Lord wants us to use to bond with Him. And the great news is that we can make this a priority within our marriages *even when devastation has occurred* if our hearts are repentant, humble, and meek.

So the bottom line is, feel the Holy Ghost with your spouse! Read the Book of Mormon together. Pray together. Teach your children and friends the gospel together. Plan dates where you know the Holy Ghost will thrive, especially if your spouse's shame is making him unreceptive to things like scriptures and prayers. Put yourselves in places and circumstances where you can learn together the very gospel truths that will lead to the deliverance of your marriage from the entrapment of Satan.

Whatever you end up doing together, point out that you are feeling the Holy Ghost, then make sure to let him know that you are enjoying feeling that with him—something that reminds him you're doing it together. Hold hands as you partake of the sacrament. Give him an encouraging smile as you watch him try to teach rowdy toddlers about Captain Moroni before bed. Write a note of gratitude on the bathroom mirror saying how much you enjoyed feeling the Spirit with him during last night's date. Kneel next to each other, shoulders touching, while you pray as a family.

These seemingly tiny acts of unity have the power to soften hearts—yours and his. That way, the Spirit that you are trying to feel together can penetrate the hardness, animosity, and pride Satan is trying so tirelessly to keep alive between you.

******

One of the things Luke and I have really enjoyed doing to draw closer to each other through the Holy Ghost is getting involved with the missionaries in our ward. We have them over for dinner often and discuss the Lord's work. We get to know their investigators by forming friendships with them and taking them to church when needed. We attend lessons on a regular basis and also have lessons in our home. We pray for them. We pray for the Lord to bless us with courage to share the gospel with those around us in hopes that we might find more people for the missionaries to teach.

We set goals together on how to act on that desire. We role-play what to say to specific people to invite them to learn more about the gospel. In essence, we have truly become each other's tagless missionary companions.

One Saturday night, Luke stayed home to put the kids to bed so I could go to the stake center an hour away and watch a women's conference with a group of ladies from Relief Society. As I sat watching, I was caught off guard by a text message from him letting me know he relapsed after the kids were asleep. We talked about it a little when I got home but I was so bothered, frustrated, and annoyed that I didn't share my true feelings with him or the Lord for days. I became short in my responses and was shutting down emotionally. Luke was left in the wake of my frustration to try to stay out of his shame as best as he could.

When I finally did open up to Luke about my feelings one evening, our heated conversation was interrupted by a lesson we had previously scheduled to go to with the missionaries. Needless to say, we did not want to go. But we went out of obligation.

It was a lesson with a new investigator we had never met. We sat on the floor of her nearly empty apartment, listening to her tell us how she came to want to meet with the missionaries. She was a nonmember and her husband was less active. They started going to church just before he was deployed, and she and her pregnant belly had to stay behind. When he returned, she said he was a different person and had confessed to having two affairs, one of which was still going on. She moved to our area to be near her parents, but unfortunately, they didn't prove to be the support she had hoped for. After they told her she deserved what had happened, she knew the only one she could truly rely on was the Savior.

My heart softened with each word. Luke and I scooted closer to each other as we listened to her testify of how the Book of Mormon had been what helped her see things clearly. Reading it chased away the darkness that had surrounded her. The love and forgiveness she had for those who hurt her was inspiring. We were there to teach her, but really she taught us in our time of hidden pain.

Feeling connected to each other once again through the Holy Ghost, Luke and I held hands on the drive home as we talked—*really* talked. I wondered how differently our night would have gone if we hadn't been in a situation where we could feel the Holy Ghost together. We surely weren't feeling it at home that night. I am so grateful for God's intervention. Had we not gone to the lesson, we might have missed that experience of healing where a huge piece of shrapnel came out cleanly for us both.

After years of practice, we have found that when we try to connect spiritually on a consistent basis, our conversations, thoughts, and actions are more in tune with each other and with the Lord. The way we think about one another and our situation is more hope-filled and compassionate. We are kinder, gentler, and more humble. It is when we stop connecting in this way that Satan seems to gain ground in the battle for our marriage and when our attachment is most at risk.

I Can Be Filled with This Love

At times, it didn't feel possible to have the oxygen of love flow within our marriage, especially when I struggled with negative thoughts, feelings, and a desire to control my husband's actions. I searched high and low for a phrase, scripture, or quote strong enough to remind me of my ability to combat Satan with the love I *could* show Luke. When I found what spoke to me, I wrote it down, taped it to my mirror, and tried to internalize it: If I cleave unto charity, Heavenly Father will fill me with *His* love for Luke.

> 45 And charity suffereth long, and is kind, and envieth not, and is not puffed up, seeketh not her own, is not easily provoked, thinketh no evil, and rejoiceth not in iniquity but rejoiceth in the truth, beareth all things, believeth all things, hopeth all things, endureth all things.
>
> 46 Wherefore, my beloved brethren, if ye have not charity, ye are nothing, for charity never faileth. Wherefore, *cleave unto charity*, which is the greatest of all, for all things must fail—
>
> 47 But charity is the pure love of Christ, and it endureth forever; and whoso is found possessed of it at the last day, it shall be well with him.
>
> 48 Wherefore, my beloved brethren, pray unto the Father with all the energy of heart, *that ye may be filled with this love*, which he hath bestowed upon all who are true followers of his Son, Jesus Christ; that ye may become the sons of God; that when he shall appear we shall be like him, for we shall see him as he is; that we may have this hope; that we may be purified even as he is pure. Amen. (Moroni 7:45–48; emphasis added)

I can pray to be filled with Christlike love for my husband. Doing so puts my mind and heart in a place to receive the love the Lord bestows upon me for him. It allows the Lord to guide us both in making and holding beneficial boundaries, in praying for and serving each other, and in bonding through shared spiritual experiences. With time I hope all will come to find, as we have, that charity really doesn't fail. Seeking after it sanctifies spouses, even those struggling with this horrible evil.

14
I can face this evil with my spouse

THE DAY LUKE AND I WERE MARRIED, THE SEALER STOOD US NEXT TO each other on the same side of the altar. Our shoulders were touching and we were holding each other's hands tightly. He told us to look into the large mirror that was purposefully placed directly across from another large mirror behind us. It was a sacred sight. I saw myself standing next to my new, official husband. I was glowing. I felt radiant, inside and out.

Then I looked at Luke in the mirror. He stood tall. He looked strong. I was so happy standing in my eternal place at his side. The smile on his face and the tears forming in his eyes told me he was feeling the same way.

Then I noticed that with both mirrors facing each other, the image of us standing together seemed to go on forever. This symbolized the eternal nature of our marital covenant, future posterity, and the ongoing joy that was now possible for us.

As we gazed into our breathtakingly beautiful future, the sealer pointed out that the image only went on forever if we looked at our spouse in the mirror. When I would shift my attention back to myself, I could no longer see the endless pattern the mirrors created. I only saw myself.

"Let this guide the focus of your marriage," the sealer said with great tenderness and love. "Look outside yourself to love and care for the other."

******

Late one night about six years later, I curled up on our couch and cried. Luke and our kids were asleep. I was alone. The living room was only lit by the moonlight shining through the very large, old windows of our third-floor historic apartment. This panic attack was the result of a series of Luke's recent relapses. After I was able to stop crying long enough to catch my breath, the Spirit brought to my mind the sacred memory of us standing together in front of the mirrors when we were married.

In that moment, my pain and anger changed the memory and inserted pornography standing between us. It was an awful sight to behold but reflected what I had felt for so long. Our marriage was meant to be as heavenly as it was in the temple that day, but it had been perverted.

Suddenly the Spirit took back control of the image. He moved the pornography from in between us to *in front of us*. He pushed our shoulders back together so they were touching again. I felt strengthened as I understood His message: face and combat all the evils of Satan, including this, *together*.

It wasn't Luke's sole responsibility, nor was it mine. We were sealed for time and all eternity, and from then on, we became one in the eyes of God. I knew we could move forward together, taking our eyes off of ourselves in the mirror and looking at and loving each other.

The cycle of frequent recurrent relapses despite our efforts (especially Luke's efforts) to be obedient, righteous, and clean was what brought me to that couch in tears. I felt defeated and I knew he did too. But with this image of us in the temple vibrant in my mind, the

Lord also brought back to my remembrance several revelatory experiences we had had over the years. He taught me truths that debunked Satan's lies and filled me with hope. I felt reassured that He would continue to guide us. We would eventually find complete healing and deliverance.

Even with sacred moments of spiritual enlightenment like this, there were still times when it felt counterintuitive to turn to an "addicted" husband for attachment because of all the disconnection that occurred. But when Luke and I realized we both were damaged by this evil, we were able to shift our focus to each other in the mirror so we could connect and heal together.

Connection Puts It in Front Instead of between Us

About two years later, the day after the trash can panic attack and subsequent epiphany about how shrapnel is removed, I was praying and pondering while lying on the couch. It was early in the morning. Luke and our three kids were still asleep. I desperately needed the Savior's light. Luke had been really stuck in his shame since relapsing while he was on his work trip. He was in a dark place and so was I.

After soaking up the calm and stillness of the early morning, I got back into our bed. Luke was awake reading. I lay down on my side with my back toward him, and the words gently trickled out of my mouth: "Why is my pain not enough for you to stop?"

He sat there silently for a few minutes and then got up to get ready for work. Before he left, he knelt down next to my side of the bed, put his hand on my shoulder, and said, "It is enough." Without opening my eyes, I whispered, "It doesn't feel like it is."

It wasn't meant to shame him. I did feel hurt, but I wasn't using that as a tool of manipulation or control to get him to change his behavior. I had tried that in the past, so I could tell this felt different.

I was just so broken. And while pondering with the Spirit on the couch, I handed that brokenness over to the Lord. Feeling attached to the Savior, I was able to talk to Luke from a place of authenticity instead of anger, panic, or fear.

Even still, I couldn't look at him. I knew that if our eyes met, I would start to cry. He took in my words, stood up, and left for work.

Over the course of the day, I developed an intense vulnerability hangover.[46] I reverted back to negative, fear-based emotions. I felt anxious and angry. It was the result of putting my raw emotions out there and having that vulnerability *not* end in connection. The first free moment I had in a morning filled with cute but demanding toddlers, I grabbed my journal and took my hangover to its pages:

> I'm in a really bad place right now emotionally. I'm so sad about where my marriage is at and overwhelmed to think about what the future holds. It could be worse, and that's part of my emotional turmoil. There's a side of me that wants to minimize this all and just say, "Put your chin up and keep moving forward—it'll all work out because Luke's an amazing guy." But I've been doing that for eight years now. He's tried to overcome this mainly on his own with good but inconsistent help from others, and it obviously hasn't really helped. I mean, it *has* helped—he's improved—but it's at a pace I don't know if I can take anymore. He's still relapsing and I'm just left here to try not to be too broken throughout the process while I struggle to muddle through the rest of life—motherhood especially.
>
> You know, we shouldn't call it relapsing. We should call it what it really is: breaking our sealing covenant. Maybe that will help him see the damage this is doing to me and to our marriage. Maybe it'll light a fire under him to pick up the pace and stop putting us through this. I feel like my insides are torn apart from the ups and downs, and I try to go on as if nothing is happening.
>
> How can he keep doing this? How can he not be taking this more seriously?! His words and actions sometimes tell me he takes it seriously. But mostly what they tell me is that he desperately wants to stop, just not enough to get over how overwhelming the effort of recovery is to him. When he doesn't stick to goals, it makes him feel bad, so he copes by ignoring that he's struggling. Life is good in his denial until he is tempted and his compulsions take over once again. He knows he does this cycle. He said it himself: "It's too overwhelming!"

---

46. Brené Brown, "The Power of Vulnerability," TED, June 2010, https://www.ted.com/talks/brene_brown_the_power_of_vulnerability?subtitle=en.

This morning I asked him why my pain is not enough for him to stop. What I meant was, Why is the thought of what this does to me and to our marriage and to his relationship with God not more overwhelming than the thought of working on his recovery?

I know I need to set a boundary, but I don't know what boundary to set. All I know is that I cannot go on like this. Why do I open myself up and try to get close to him? I'm just setting myself up for worse pain!

I need someone to tell me what boundary to set. Please, Father in Heaven, tell me what to do. The part of me that wants to minimize this is telling me that I'm being selfish and melodramatic. Please, provide some clarity and companionship. I'm so confused and alone.

I felt a little better after that entry. Then, in the afternoon, I had a sudden desire to reach out to Luke. I texted him but knew he had already had his lunch break and wouldn't see my message until after work. I sent it anyway. I wanted to act on the desire to connect to him while I still had it. As I typed, an idea developed that hadn't occurred to me until that moment: I suggested we set aside a night every week to study and discuss something together like the Church's Family Services Addiction Recovery Program manual.[47]

Luke went straight from work to a church meeting, and when he got home that night, he told me how glad he was that I shared my raw emotions with him that morning. He said that when I did, something hit him and he couldn't get "Why is my pain not enough?" out of his head the entire day.

During his lunch break, he went for a walk outside and prayed for guidance. He said he felt impressed to read the Church's Family Services Addiction Recovery Program manual. As he read, he realized his life had become unmanageable and his efforts to do it on his own had not worked. The pain of the problem had become more painful than the pain of the solution. He felt like studying that manual regularly and discussing it with me was the next step the Lord would have

---

47. "Addiction Recovery Program Guide," The Church of Jesus Christ of Latter-day Saints, accessed Aug. 22, 2024, https://addictionrecovery.churchofjesuschrist.org/addiction-recovery-program-guide?lang=eng.

him take to work toward deliverance and healing. He had studied the manual before, but he said now his heart felt more open to it.

Having the same impression separately, as we sought out the Lord's direction, was confirmation of His involvement in our lives. He loves us and wants to help. After acting on His direction, we discovered the reason behind His prompting: to change our association with talking about Luke's struggle.

Changing Our Discussions about It

Up to that point, which was about eight years into marriage, almost every time we talked about Luke's sexual sins or my pain from his choices, it was because he relapsed. We unknowingly made talking about recovery its own trigger—a fear trigger for me and a shame trigger for Luke. We associated that topic of conversation so much with those negative emotions that talking about it always led to further disconnection. The main exception was when we were in therapy at the beginning of our marriage. But even then, Luke was so closed off and I was so injured that our discussions were still filled with shame and fear.

The Lord knew that if we were going to face this evil together, we had to be able to talk about it *together*. With Him guiding our efforts, and Luke taking the initiative to plan and execute it, we started setting aside one night a week to focus on the healing of our marriage—to recover it. We called it "Recovery Night." We made it a priority. We put it on our calendars and never scheduled anything else during that time.

Each week we tried to allow the Spirit to guide what we did during those nights after the kids were in bed. Sometimes that meant listening to an uplifting, relevant podcast and discussing it. Other times we read from the Church's addiction recovery manual, supportive websites,[48] the scriptures, or general conference talks together. These gave our conversations a clear focus. As we let the Spirit lead us to the

---

48. See "Life Help | Pornography," The Church of Jesus Christ of Latter-day Saints, accessed Aug. 22, 2024, https://www.churchofjesuschrist.org/study/life-help/pornography?lang=eng.

material we studied, it allowed Him to guide our discussions. And so line upon line, week after week, we received the enlightenment and guidance we needed.

We very quickly started looking forward to those nights when we could talk, connect, and learn together. It felt like a breath of fresh air to, for the first time, talk about those difficult things consistently without being in the immediate aftermath of an explosion. Because Luke was still relapsing, some recovery nights I *was* in that aftermath, but not *every* recovery night, which became the point.

With time, I began to notice a healthy shift within my mind. Before, the disconnection caused by his relapses *and talking about* his relapses would overpower any connection we experienced in between relapses. So for the majority of our marriage, I viewed those painful experiences as consistent and our moments of connection as occasional. But with the weekly uplifting discussions, I started to see our nights of connection as the constant and his relapses as the variable. This shift made it so much more clear to us both that lust, in all its forms, is the enemy—an enemy we were finally facing together.

One of the resources the Spirit led us to because of our Recovery Nights was a new support group for those who struggle with sex addiction. Luke had recently started practicing mindfulness consistently through his changed eating habits, and in this new group, he was able to deepen that understanding and truly unlock the liberating power of being mindful. He started doing "dailies" again, which are daily recovery goals like journaling, meditating, exercising, and connecting to the Lord. He created the habit of checking in with himself about his feelings with the Feelings Wheel and then sharing those feelings.

Prior to this, dailies overwhelmed him. When he wouldn't stick to his daily goals, he would shame himself into an all-or-nothing mentality. Not being able to be perfect made him not want to try them at all.

For the first time, though, the focus of his recovery to-do list changed. Instead of constantly trying to reach sobriety through a long checklist of preventative measures, he realized it was more effective to use his dailies to stay mindful of his feelings. That was the purpose of them—to keep him present and aware instead of in a mindless state at the mercy of his need to escape. If he let them, dailies would help him be in a better position to use his agency the way he really wanted to when temptation came. It was self-discipline truly fueled by a desire to act instead of being acted upon.

Between our Recovery Nights, his support group, and the mindfulness he was practicing, it felt like the graveclothes Luke's struggle had him wrapped in were really coming off. He seemed happy. He took charge and led our weekly studies. That was very healing for me. He was also willing to be vulnerable and share hard things about his past during our discussions. He accepted my empathy and used it to work toward his own healing.

Learning to empathize with one another was one of the hardest parts of looking at *each other* instead of looking at *ourselves* in the mirror. But over time and with consistency, it became more natural and instinctive. We experienced for ourselves what President Gordon B. Hinckley taught: "True love is not so much a matter of romance as it is a matter of anxious concern for the well being of one's companion."[49]

A light started to shine in his eyes. I could tell he felt empowered and capable, not because he was doing it on his own but because he was allowing himself to *not* do it on his own. The time between relapses became longer than ever before, and his behavior toward me grew more tender by the day. With him now consistently connecting to himself, to others, and to the Lord, and me doing the same, we started connecting with each other on a beautifully deep level.

It was a significant turning point for us.

---

49. Gordon B. Hinckley, "Except the Lord Build the House," *Ensign*, May 1971, 71.

15
I can see my husband through God's eyes

Shortly after Luke and I were married, I had a dream. In it, I was running away from a man. I didn't know who he was, but I knew my life was in grave danger. I was so afraid and completely panicked. Suddenly my grandma, who passed away when I was a baby, appeared in front of me. It stopped me dead in my tracks. She stood, beautiful, happy, and glowing with a smile on her lovely face. She didn't seem afraid or hurried at all as she said, "Elizabeth, Luke is a *good* man." Her peaceful eyes told me how pleased she was with who I chose to marry. I wrote that dream down in my journal, but time and pain quickly faded the memory of it.

******

Our little family lives in a town that was hit hard by Hurricane Florence. Our house was surprisingly untouched by this destructive storm. We knew that was a blessing from the Lord that put us in a position to help our community rebuild. We spent months mucking out moldy, flooded homes and cleaning up what uprooted trees left in their wake. Because our kids were too small to volunteer, Luke and I would switch off. One of us would stay home with them while the other went out to help. It was a tender time of life that brought with it many welcome changes.

We had started doing our Recovery Nights just a couple of months before Florence came. We enjoyed connecting in that way so much that we didn't let her stop our routine. One of the blessings that came from volunteering was a selfless attitude. It filled our lives and spilled over into our Recovery Nights. During one of those nights, about a month after the hurricane, Luke shared something from his past that was extremely difficult for me to hear.

As we talked, King David from the Old Testament came to my mind. I thought it was strange since I was not that familiar with him. I knew the major details of his story but didn't understand why he of all people would come to mind, especially since I probably hadn't read or thought about him in years. What I did remember about King David, though, wasn't very good, and that confused me even more. Was the Lord telling me Luke was just like him?

The next night, I started feeling very uneasy. Luke had signed up to volunteer with hurricane relief, so after the kids were in bed, I used that alone time to take my concerns to my journal.

> Last night Luke and I had a wonderful, long talk after listening to a podcast about fear triggers. It led to a discussion about sexual experiences we've had in the past that we feel shame around. We both opened up about things buried deep down. It was really therapeutic and bonding.
>
> But since then, I've felt more withdrawn and afraid. It almost feels like disclosure of a relapse. I feel caught off guard, like this is uncharted territory. I'm not really sure how to process it all. The things he told me are things he has never told me before. Some of them make me feel like what I thought was reality—and who I

> thought he's been for years and years—really isn't the case. I just feel confused and afraid, I guess. I thought I knew him, but do I really?
>
> I know now that this is a very common thought process in the wives of those who struggle with pornography. Whether she discovers his behavior on her own or if he discloses it to her, the betrayal she feels can convince her that she doesn't know who he is. She can wonder if she's been wrong about him the whole time. Suddenly her world feels upside down and she subconsciously starts questioning his intention behind things he's done throughout their relationship: "Did he really mean this?" "Is he really like that?" It's overwhelming. Almost suffocating. She doesn't know what to think of him, so to try to protect herself from future surprises, her fear tells her to think the worst.
>
> I'm afraid that I'm thinking the worst.

I closed my journal and said a prayer for guidance, but I didn't receive peace or answers. So I drew a bubble bath and grabbed my favorite bath companion: the *Ensign*. As I opened the front cover to scan the table of contents, King David came back to my mind again.

"I wish there was an article about him in here," I thought. "Maybe brushing up on his story will give me whatever I need to move through this." I decided then that I'd pull out the Old Testament after my bath to find out.

Feeling the warm water flow from the faucet onto my feet, I started scanning the table of contents of the *Ensign* for an article to read as I soaked. And then I saw it: "What We Can Learn from King David's Fall."[50] My jaw almost hit the bottom of the tub. I quickly flipped to the listed page as my smile almost turned into an audible giggle. This was no coincidence. Its preciseness and remarkable timing had the Savior's name written all over it. I knew it was from Him and that it would address the things I wondered about Luke.

Sure enough, reading it provided me with the exact answers, understanding, and guidance I needed. I learned the Lord's perspective. I saw Luke through His eyes instead of through my fear-driven view.

---

50. Frank F. Judd Jr., "What We Can Learn from King David's Fall," *Ensign*, Oct. 2018, 54–57.

As I read, I could see clearly how differently Luke and King David handled their decisions. Instead of dwelling on his wrong choices from the past, I was empowered by the Spirit to see *how Luke reacted* to those choices and how he continues his efforts today.

When Luke got home later that night, I ran up to him and wrapped my arms around him. He put his arms around me and we breathed in each other's familiar scent. Granted, his scent did have more of a mustiness after such hard work, but it was still him.

After several moments of closeness, I pulled slightly out of the hug to look into his eyes. My fear told me to look one last time for something—anything that would contradict what the Lord had just taught me about him. But all I could see was the man I married. He was more experienced, older, and much wiser. But really, he was still the Luke I had always known.

Then the image of my grandma came to my mind as I remembered, probably for the first time since having it, my dream from so long ago.

"Yes, yes," I thought to myself, "I know this man. He's Luke—my husband, my friend. He *is* a good man."

******

A few days later, I was reading in 1 Nephi. I've read Lehi's dream many times throughout my life; this, however, was the first time I ever realized that he was in darkness at the beginning of his dream. How did I miss that in my many years of scripture study and seminary? It was only *after* he prayed to the Lord because of such darkness that he saw the tree of life and received all the understanding that came with it (see 1 Nephi 8:7–9).

Then my thoughts turned from the tree of life to the First Vision. It played like a movie in my mind, and I noticed the same pattern. That beautiful pillar of light descended only after Joseph Smith cried out to the Lord for deliverance from the darkness that attacked him (see Joseph Smith—History 1:15–17).

In that moment, I felt connected to these two beloved prophets of God. I didn't receive a vision significant to the whole world like they did. But I did receive one significant to *my* whole world.

God's Opportunity

Like Lehi and Joseph, I was in darkness. I was confused. I was lost and entangled in fear. And like them, God tenderly responded to my plea for intervention with light and understanding. I still had pieces of shrapnel surface the following weeks, but I was able to remove them with the experiences the Lord had blessed me with that night in the bubble bath with my *Ensign*.

To all who are struggling with the confusion caused by the discovery and disclosure of a spouse's inappropriate sexual behavior, know that the Savior can and will chase away the darkness that is consuming you. Reach out to Him with your words, actions, and broken heart. You *can* see your situation and your spouse through His eyes.

And when you do, you might be surprised by the good man He shows you.

16
I can keep my covenants

I THINK SOME PEOPLE END THEIR MARRIAGES FAR TOO RASHLY, especially when they have children. I understand why they do it; they're hurting, want to be happy, and think they only can be by escaping the difficulty or injustices of their circumstances. It doesn't help that society encourages this mentality. The goal to live a pain-free, self-indulgent, live-for-the-moment life has almost become an obsession today.

Truly, we all deserve to be happy, but does being happy mean we should live without suffering? Or is *the suffering* part of *the happy*?

During moments of my own deep anguish, when I have been tempted to rashly end my marriage, I have had to remind myself to slow down and broaden my perspective. Nothing helps one do this quite like rereading what God told Joseph Smith when he was in Liberty Jail. After listing many different hypothetical ways Joseph could suffer immensely, He added a few more:

And if thou shouldst be cast into the pit, or into the hands of murderers, and the sentence of death passed upon thee; if thou be cast into the deep; if the billowing surge conspire against thee; if fierce winds become thine enemy; if the heavens gather blackness, and all the elements combine to hedge up the way; and above all, if the very jaws of hell shall gape open the mouth wide after thee . . .

Then He said these sobering words:

Know thou, my son, that *all* these things shall give thee experience, and shall be for thy good.

The Son of Man hath descended below them all. Art thou greater than he?

Therefore, *hold on thy way, and the priesthood shall remain with thee*; for their bounds are set, they cannot pass. Thy days are known, and thy years shall not be numbered less; therefore, fear not what man can do, for God shall be with you forever and ever. (Doctrine and Covenants 122:7–9; emphasis added)

Hold On Thy Way

One day, I attended an endowment session at the temple. I was completely heartbroken because—you guessed it—Luke had relapsed again.

I settled into my seat to wait for the session to begin and looked around the room at the awe-inspiring, beautiful floor-to-ceiling murals. As I did, a few women also attending the session caught my eye.

First, there was a young woman participating in a live ordinance with her mom as her escort. The little paper tag pinned to her dress told me it was her first time making these particular covenants.

Behind them sat a middle-aged woman with special needs. Her sister came in with her and helped her get into her seat. They sat next to a *very* elderly woman. It honestly looked like any breath could be her last.

At one point during the session, I watched the mom helping her daughter through this new experience. They were both beaming as she whispered gentle guidance into her daughter's ear.

At the same time, I saw the middle-aged woman with special needs. I could tell she had been to the temple many times and knew what to do but physically needed help doing it. As soon as her sister was finished helping her, she turned to the very elderly woman and noticed she needed help as well. Although they didn't seem to know one another, she cheerfully helped her.

This whole scene brought me to tears. I felt like I was watching the Father's plan for our mortal journey unfold before my eyes.

First was the new daughter in her infancy on the covenant path, who needed help because of a lack of experience and understanding yet was glowing with excitement and discovery. I remembered that feeling—it is absolutely amazing.

Next, there was the middle-aged woman with disabilities. She had the experience and understanding required yet found herself needing significant help because of the limitations of mortality. She simply couldn't do it on her own, which led me to realize that every one of us has our own unique mortal limitations that put us in this same position of needing help. She radiated perseverance, patience, and determination. "This," I thought to myself, "is the phase I'm trying to find my stride in now."

Lastly was the elderly woman on death's door. It was evident that she was full of experience and understanding from years of Christlike discipleship. It was as if she had run a spiritual marathon and was coming to her final steps—painful final steps, which prompted the needed help.

What a remarkable feeling it must be to get to that point and find yourself so at home in the house of the Lord that you come even when it's difficult and you'd have every excuse not to. When I get to that point in my own marathon, and all along the way, I want to be just as dependable in the Lord's eyes as I bet this woman was.

Suddenly I noticed an elderly man across the room. He was constantly looking back and over at the elderly woman. "Aha!" I thought with a smile. "Of course, her husband!" You could tell by the way he looked at her. There was love and admiration there but also worry. It was obviously taking everything he had not to jump up and go help his wife himself!

With that, my thoughts turned to Luke. My aching heart longed to be his the way this elderly woman was her husband's. I wondered, "Will Luke be there with me when I'm the very elderly woman?" Fear and confusion about the future started to overtake me.

And then, with a gentleness that I've only experienced from the Holy Ghost, my focus was brought back to those few women I noticed moments earlier. The eternal progress they symbolized is what *I can control* in my circumstances. "Jesus Christ," the Spirit reminded me, "will take care of the rest." Or in other words, "Hold on thy way, and the priesthood [which is literally God's power][51] shall remain with thee" (Doctrine and Covenants 122:9).

Because of that and other sacred communication from the Lord, I've discovered this empowering truth: If *I* keep the covenants *I* made at baptism, in the endowment, *and at my sealing*, I will be exalted and receive every promised blessing, no matter how Luke chooses to use his agency.

In the April 2024 general conference, Elder Matthew L. Carpenter clarified this empowering and incredibly vital point:

> If you remain faithful to the covenants you made when you were endowed, you will receive the personal blessings promised to you in the endowment *even if your spouse has broken his or her covenants or withdrawn from the marriage.* If you were sealed and later divorced, and if your sealing is not canceled, the personal blessings of that sealing remain in effect for you if you remain faithful. . . .
>
> If you are concerned that you will somehow be tied to an unrepentant former spouse, remember, *you will not!* God will not require anyone to remain in a sealed relationship throughout eternity against his or her will. Heavenly Father will ensure that we will receive every blessing that our desires and choices allow.
>
> However, if a cancellation of sealing is desired, agency is respected. Certain procedures can be followed. *But this should not be done casually!* . . . It is important to understand that to receive the blessings of exaltation, we must demonstrate that we are willing

---

51. "The Priesthood Is God's Power," *Liahona*, Aug. 2021.

to enter into and faithfully keep this new and everlasting covenant, either in this life or the next.[52]

Receiving the Help We Need to Hold On Our Way

In Matthew 11, the Savior entreats us: "Come unto me, all ye that labour and are heavy laden, and I will give you rest. Take my yoke upon you, and learn of me; for I am meek and lowly in heart: and ye shall find rest unto your souls. For my yoke is easy, and my burden is light" (verses 28–30).

A yoke is a wooden beam with two attached harnesses. It's placed upon the shoulders and necks of two strong animals, like oxen, connecting them together. Its purpose is to spread the weight being pulled between the animals so they can more easily accomplish the task at hand.

This scriptural invitation is often quoted as a beautiful reminder that when we're yoked *to the Savior*, He as one ox and us as the other, we can pull the burdens of our life side by side with Him. But let's read the beginning of verse 29 again and perhaps see an alternate meaning:

"Take *my* yoke upon you . . ."

When two oxen are yoked together, is it one of the oxen who owns the yoke? No, the *master of the oxen* owns the yoke and places it upon the two animals. He stands with them, guiding, directing, and encouraging them as *they* work, yoked to each other with *his* yoke upon them.

Can you picture it? Jesus Christ, the owner, stands ready to put two willing oxen to work in His field with the help His yoke provides. When Luke and I entered into the new and everlasting covenant, Christ put us to work *with His yoke placed upon us*. Only with that yoke, He promised, would we find rest unto our souls, for His yoke is easy and his burden light.

But with how difficult the work has been, how could Christ possibly use such adjectives as *easy* and *light*? From our viewpoint as the

---

52. Matthew L. Carpenter, "Fruit That Remains," *Liahona*, May 2024, 63–64; emphasis added.

oxen, we cannot see all that our Master can see. Only as we move along and press forward do we begin to understand the big picture: we are not only refining this field, but by working it with His yoke on our shoulders, He is refining us. It is that very yoke that strengthens us to meet the challenge because when we take His yoke upon us, we take *Him* upon us—His perspective, His love, His power, and all the effects of His atoning sacrifice.

Choose Your Hard

There have been times I've felt so confused about the future of my marriage that I wondered if it'd be best to just take the yoke off us. Was the Master even still standing there to guide us as we try to work our field? With Joseph, I have cried, "O God, where art thou? And where is the pavilion that covereth thy hiding place?" (Doctrine and Covenants 121:1). But that wasn't because God left me—it was because I distanced myself from Him (see Doctrine and Covenants 3:8; Alma 36:3).

In our earthly suffering, we have two choices (see 2 Nephi 2:27). We can allow pain and festering shrapnel to harden our hearts toward God and others. Or we can patiently give Him the opportunity to lead us on the path He knows will be the most refining, bringing with it true happiness.

Honestly, both choices are hard. So choose your hard.

You *can* have His help in knowing how to accurately evaluate your circumstances, but it will require intentional sacrifice on your part. President Russell M. Nelson has shared specific directions outlining how to secure this promised blessing:

> Every woman and every man who makes covenants with God and keeps those covenants, and who participates worthily in priesthood ordinances, *has direct access to the power of God.* Those who are endowed in the house of the Lord receive a gift of God's priesthood power by virtue of their covenant, *along with a gift of knowledge to know how to draw upon that power.* . . .
>
> I invite you to study prayerfully section 25 of the Doctrine and Covenants and discover what the Holy Ghost will teach you. Your

personal spiritual endeavor will bring you *joy* as you gain, understand, and use the power with which you have been endowed.

Part of this endeavor will require you to put aside many things of this world. Sometimes we speak almost casually about walking away from the world with its contention, pervasive temptations, and false philosophies. But truly doing so requires you to examine your life meticulously and regularly. As you do so, the Holy Ghost will prompt you about what is no longer needful, what is no longer worthy of your time and energy.

As you shift your focus away from worldly distractions, some things that seem important to you now will recede in priority. You will need to say no to some things, even though they may seem harmless. As you embark upon and continue this lifelong process of consecrating your life to the Lord, *the changes in your perspective, feelings, and spiritual strength will amaze you!*[53]

You can do it. You can keep your covenants and draw upon God's power to help you decide what to do about the yoke upon your neck and shoulders. Your eternity and that of your posterity depends on it.

Sometimes, while in the depths of despair, it can be easy to forget that the choices we make affect our children and posterity. But they are one of the reasons it's imperative to "trust in the Lord with all thine heart; and lean not unto thine own understanding" (Proverbs 3:5). And if you do so by acknowledging Him in all your ways, you are promised that "he shall direct thy paths" (verse 6). Then, with His yoke and the power given you through your covenants, you will be blessed with the courage and strength to move forward in the way He counsels you to go.

As you pray and consider these things, remember that He will never ask you to do something without there being a way for it to be done (see 1 Nephi 3:7). I know this is true because I was able to "hold on my way" when I didn't think I could, and God's power *has* remained with me. And because of that, I've been beautifully blessed with true happiness.

President Nelson taught:

---

53. Russell M. Nelson, "Spiritual Treasures," *Ensign* or *Liahona*, Nov. 2019, 77; emphasis added.

[Jesus Christ] will deliver you from your most excruciating circumstances in His own way and time. As you come unto Him in faith, He will guide, preserve, and protect you. He will heal your broken heart and comfort you in your distress. He will give you access to His power. And He will make the impossible in your life become possible.

Jesus Christ is the only enduring source of hope, peace, and joy for you. Satan can never replicate any of these. And Satan will never help you.

On the other hand, God's work and His glory is to bring about the "immortality and eternal life of man" (Moses 1:39). God will do everything He can, short of violating your agency, to help you not miss out on the greatest blessings in all eternity.

God has a special love for each person who makes a covenant with Him in the waters of baptism. And that divine love deepens as additional covenants are made and faithfully kept. Then at the end of mortal life, precious is the reunion of each covenant child with our Heavenly Father.[54]

---

54. Russell M. Nelson, "Choices for Eternity" (worldwide devotional for young adults, May 15, 2022), Gospel Library.

17
I can experience true intimacy

THE SWEET WIFE OF THE FRIEND WHO INVITED US TO INCORPORATE the Savior more into our efforts gently put her arm around me one evening when we were alone. "I know it sounds strange," she said, "but be intimate with Luke as soon as you're comfortable. Heavenly Father meant for intimacy to be a bonding experience, and that's what you'll both need."

It *was* strange advice. No one had ever told me that before. She made it seem like there was something big I was not understanding about sex.

While I was driving home from her house, I thought about the windy road our intimacy had taken over the years. A night from the early part of our marriage came to my mind.

I was lying alone on top of our made bed, too emotionally exhausted to even undo the covers. Tears streamed down my face as I sobbed uncontrollably. Anger, hopelessness, and a deep sense of loss consumed me. The tension building inside was becoming more than I could handle, and I began to scream at the top of my lungs.

"I hate sex! I hate it! I never want to do it again!"

My relatively new husband's frequent relapses and the disconnection between us broke my heart. The purity and beauty of our intimacy were *dead,* and I mourned the sexual relationship I thought we were going to have.

As time passed, I found the balance between healing psychologically and spiritually. This helped me to have a desire to be with Luke again, but I was still guarded and anxious. Many times when we were intimate, my mind would be hijacked either by images of Luke relapsing or by the low self-esteem those relapses created in me. Fear, confusion, and betrayal would take me out of that beautiful moment and I would cry.

I'm sure it was disheartening for Luke. We had made so much progress by that point in our marriage. Yet every time I cried, he would immediately stop and hold me until my tears ran out. Then he'd ask if I wanted to talk about it, making sure I knew we didn't need to continue—we could connect in another way, he'd say, a way I'd feel more comfortable with. Most times, I would gratefully choose to connect in some other way because in those moments, I wanted nothing more than to escape.

Experience Versus Escape

On March 1, 1932, the twenty-month-old first child of famous pilot Charles Lindbergh and his wife, Anne Morrow Lindbergh, was kidnapped. This kidnapping tragically resulted in their son's death. Many years later, Mrs. Lindbergh wrote, "I do not believe that sheer suffering teaches. If suffering alone taught, all the world would be wise, since everyone suffers. To suffering must be added mourning, understanding, patience, love, openness, and the willingness to remain vulnerable."[55]

---

55. Anne Morrow Lindbergh, quoted in "Historical Notes: Lindbergh Nightmare," *Time,* Feb. 5, 1973, https://time.com/archive/6840652/historical-notes-lindbergh-nightmare/.

When I noticed the hijacking of my mind becoming a pattern, I asked Luke if we could start each intimate encounter with a prayer. Despite it being a rather odd idea, he compassionately agreed.

Over the years, that simple act of literally stopping to invite the Holy Ghost into our intimacy before proceeding added "understanding, patience, love, openness, and the willingness to remain vulnerable" to my suffering. With these additions, the Spirit was able to show me that I had two choices. In those moments when darkness fell over me, I could either *escape*, which I had grown very used to doing, or I could *experience*. But experience what? I wasn't quite sure yet.

The Joy Set Before Us

Learning how to experience instead of escape is one of the skills we came to earth to gain. Escaping is what the natural man inside us defaults to in discomfort. It's also the path that Satan tempts us to go down. Escape is the foundation of my husband's battle with pornography. Now it was my turn to battle with it.

Of course, when we choose to escape, we don't think about it as escape. We do it because discomfort is too uncomfortable. We do it because it feels easy, even wise and maybe rejuvenating on the surface. But neither comfort nor peace comes from the absence of pain. They come from experiencing mortality, as Mrs. Lindbergh described. They come from remembering that "man's extremity is God's opportunity" and that because of the Atonement of Jesus Christ, "every experience can become a redemptive experience if we remain bonded to our Father in Heaven through that difficulty."[56] We can't forget what the Lord told the Prophet Joseph Smith: "All these things shall give thee *experience*, and shall be for thy good" (Doctrine and Covenants 122:7).

Jesus Christ Himself chose the path of mindful experience instead of easy escape. While describing His suffering in the Garden of Gethsemane, He said, "Which suffering caused myself, even God, the greatest of all, to tremble because of pain, and to bleed at every pore,

---

56. Jeffrey R. Holland, "Lessons from Liberty Jail" (Brigham Young University devotional, Sept. 7, 2008), 4, speeches.byu.edu.

and to suffer both body and spirit—and would that I might not drink the bitter cup, and shrink" (Doctrine and Covenants 19:18).

The thought of escaping agony crossed His mind. He didn't want to drink that bitter cup. But He also knew that if He chose not to drink it, He would shrink, and the shame that would inevitably bring would not be worth the escape. It never is. And so He said, "Nevertheless, glory be to the Father, and I partook and finished my preparations unto the children of men" (Doctrine and Covenants 19:19).

What kept Him present in His pain enough to experience what He needed to experience? Hebrews 12:2 gives us insight into His motivation. It says, "Looking unto Jesus the author and finisher of our faith; who *for the joy that was set before him* endured the cross, despising the shame, and is set down at the right hand of the throne of God" (emphasis added).

What joy was set before him?

- "Glory be to the Father": The glory and joy His Father would feel having this Atonement performed for His children.
- "Finished my preparations": The joy He would feel having finished his divine calling, making true joy possible for us and for His Father.
- "Unto the children of men": Our joy when we would be able to repent and be exalted.

After *experiencing* instead of escaping all of that suffering, He was able to later say, "My joy is full" (3 Nephi 17:20). Christ's example reminds me of these words by President Nelson: "Joy is powerful, and focusing on joy brings God's power into our lives. . . . What will you and I be able to endure as we focus on the joy that is 'set before' us? . . . What disappointments, even tragedies, will turn to our good?"[57]

With time and divine help, I felt safe to be intimately vulnerable with Luke. I felt more capable of intentionally choosing to experience whatever the Lord was trying to guide me to instead of choosing to escape. And as I did, I discovered the incredible joy set before me.

---

57. Russell M. Nelson, "Joy and Spiritual Survival," *Ensign* or *Liahona*, Nov. 2016, 83; emphasis added.

True Intimacy

One evening, after our prayer, Luke and I were feeling bonded and close. But as usual, darkness and negativity started to flow over me. This was it: another opportunity for me to choose—a chance for me to *act* as an agent and *impact* my circumstances. So in my mind, I desperately called out for help to my Heavenly Father. I hoped He would help me not ruin this moment between Luke and me with my intrusive thoughts.

Suddenly my heart and mind opened up as never before, and I went on a journey through different layers. The first was physical pleasure. This was not new—we had been married for many years at that point and had experienced this several times. The next layer was emotional connection. We had also experienced this before, although this time felt richer somehow.

Thinking that would be the extent of this experience, I was surprised when I was brought to the next layer—spiritual unity. It seemed like Luke and I had entered a holy space where our spirits could touch. I realized there that the first layer relaxed my physical body, the second relaxed my mind, and the third relaxed my spirit, all in preparation for the final layer: Jesus Christ.

Through the Holy Ghost, I was shown the negative things I was feeling and thinking about myself, and He—in the most potent way I've ever experienced—changed it all. It vanished in an instant and was replaced by the Savior's perfect, unconditional love for me. In that love, I felt what it meant to truly love myself.

Then He helped me to clearly feel and understand Luke's pure love for me. This was incredibly healing since I had doubted that love many times. But there was no room for doubt in this experience—there was only room for truth and things as they really are.

Revelations often fulfill multiple purposes. This one was no exception. Not only was it a revelation to show me how God viewed me, Luke, and our marriage, but I also learned that Satan has perverted sex more than I realized.

God means for sex to be a bonding experience between husband, wife, *and* Him. A source of revelation. A source of learning and vision.

It makes so much sense now that I see it. Intimacy is a most sacred act done in a most sacred relationship—of course it would serve as a means to commune with God! Particularly for the husband—the appointed patriarch—to *bring his wife* to where she can commune with God!

Her husband is the only one who can do this in this way. No other person on earth can give his wife this experience! It requires dedication, patience, humility, selflessness, and the Spirit of God to bring her there. It requires a true, celestial bond that is attentively cared for and nourished by both husband and wife.

Why didn't I see it before? Because Satan truly has perverted it. He has marketed intimacy as an act of lust that offends the Spirit, thus keeping people from passing through the necessary layers. Many stay at the top layer of physical pleasure or reach the second of emotional connection. But just like every other counterfeit that Satan creates, this also comes up short when compared to what God intends for His children to experience.

I am grateful to my Savior for waiting for me underneath all those layers, for answering our prayers, and for mending this heart of mine that is so often troubled. Incredibly, once I encountered the resurrected Savior in this way, the beauty and purity of our intimacy were resurrected too.

18
I can help others

A POWERFUL TRUTH THAT NOW SOOTHES MY SOUL IS THAT OUR EXtremity has put us in a position to help others in a loving, authentic, and effective way. One of the most important things we've found that we can do is to initiate conversations and be a supportive, empathetic person for someone else.

Pornography, however often it's viewed, thrives in secrecy. Shame nags those who struggle to remain in the shadows. But often, deep down, they want someone to know about it. It's a heavy burden to carry all alone.

Once, I was visiting with a loved one. Our conversation ended, and as I was leaving the room, I felt impressed to stop, turn around, and ask him if he had ever been exposed to pornography. I was taken off guard by this thought because it had nothing to do with anything we had been talking about. He also didn't know about Luke's struggle with it, so this question would seem out of left field for many reasons. But two things I had learned up to that point in my life encouraged me to act on the thought.

First, I know how the Holy Ghost speaks to me. I knew this was a prompting from the Spirit because it felt like other promptings I had previously had many times about other things. I also had learned to *never* postpone a prompting.[58]

Second, depending on the level of involvement, I knew that for some, just bringing the issue out into the open can be the healing balm needed for them to stop viewing. And if there was a deeper involvement going on, then I knew he'd need support.

And so, with these two thoughts building up my courage, I did as the Spirit directed: I stopped, turned around, and just asked. It was simple. It was clear. It was very direct. Most importantly, it was done completely out of love.

We stood there in silence as I watched his eyes well up with tears. We then had a beautiful, heartfelt conversation about the specific struggles in our lives. We bonded. We supported one another. And in that moment, the Lord blessed us with an awareness of His infinite love for us both.

On another occasion, I dropped by a friend's house one afternoon. She and I were in the beginning stages of our friendship, and although we felt like kindred spirits, we didn't know each other very well.

During our conversation, however, she shared with me that her husband struggled with what she referred to as a pornography addiction. She seemed completely broken and beside herself. As I listened, I felt the Holy Ghost enlighten my mind and guide me to know how best to respond. I watched the beautiful change that occurred in her countenance because of my simple, empathetic responses. It was especially meaningful for me to be able to give to someone else the very thing I needed. From that conversation and many that have followed, she and I have been able to be there for each other through incredibly hard things.

******

Because of the heartache that lust has caused in our lives, Luke and I know how important it is to help others talk about their own

---

58. See Thomas S. Monson, "The Spirit Giveth Life," *Ensign*, May 1985, 70.

feelings and experiences. We know the damage that can be done by minimizing or degrading those who struggle or who have questions. The most effective way to talk about lust in all its forms is to do so plainly and directly; with an intent to love and support, not to gossip, judge, or shame; and with the Lord's help when moved upon by the Holy Ghost. This is especially true with our children.

One day, I couldn't find our three-year-old son, Hyrum, anywhere in the house. When I went to look in his room, the door was locked. I unlocked and opened the door to find him exploring his naked body. I knew that a lot of kids that age go through an exploratory phase, but I also knew this was an opportunity to instill, even at such a young age, eternal truths that would serve him well throughout his life.

Luke and I try to teach our children in the same pattern the Lord uses with us: teach doctrine, invite to act, and promise blessings.[59] So I dove right in. As age-appropriate as possible, we talked about the body, who created it, how They ask us to treat and care for it, and why.

We had a good conversation and he put his clothes back on. I felt like a very successful parent if I do say so myself.

Ten minutes later, I found his door locked again. Fear and discouragement washed over me. I wasn't sure what to do or where to go from there. We ended up having the same conversation, and it happened several more times.

When Luke got home that night, I filled him in. I told him I knew our son was really little but that the day's events triggered so much of my fear. Part of me worried I was overreacting because of my betrayal trauma and what our marriage had been through. Another part of me worried I was underreacting and needed to take immediate action to prevent my innocent child from having the same difficulties Luke had. I cried and cried and cried. I felt the weight of all of my children's current and future happiness on my shoulders but also felt powerless to help them obtain it.

Luke hugged me. Then he put his hand on mine and gave me a reassuring smile. "It makes complete sense that you feel that. But

---

59. Scott Taylor, "Learn Elder Bednar's pattern for studying conference messages — doctrine, invitations, blessings." *Church News*, Mar. 25, 2021.

remember," he said, "you are not doing this alone and neither are they. None of us are. I will talk with him in the morning when he wakes up." We prayed that night about it, and in the morning, Luke talked with Hyrum, man to little man.

I stood just outside the door so I could hear their conversation. It was one of the most beautiful moments I've experienced as a parent and also as a wounded wife. I listened to Luke speak *with* Hyrum. It was simple and gentle. He spoke with a love and understanding that I suspect is only possible from a man who knows firsthand the difficulties he was talking about.

The short but tender conversation ended with Luke saying, "I'm going to wear my clothes all day today and take care of my body the way Jesus asked us to. I know that will make me happy. I want you to be happy too. Will you wear your clothes with me today?"

I heard Hyrum excitedly respond, "Yeah Dad! Let's do it! Best buddies!"

After that, we had many of those same conversations with Hyrum, one-on-one and with both of us together. Prayerfully, we learned that repetition with patience is key. At times it felt monotonous to us as adults, but I don't think it did to him. After each conversation, it seemed to sink in a little bit more.

Sometime later, while Hyrum was coloring with our youngest daughter, I overheard him telling her in his three-year-old way that Jesus made our bodies special and that we'll be happy if we treat them the way He asks us to. Because we've had the same conversations with our older daughter, she joined him in teaching our youngest.

This is how Heavenly Father intends for this loving cycle to go: We struggle, we learn, and then we help others who go on to help others too. As wives, we can feel that our explosive marriages and shrapnel-filled bodies are injustices we should never have had to endure. But I know that the Savior can take those injustices and make them a sacred education for us and for our husbands; an education that our children and loved ones can benefit from; and an education that God can use to reach His precious children.

Turn Them to Christ

With years of consistent effort and hard work, Luke and I began to heal. That healing brought emotional, spiritual, and physical energy as well as a desire to help others.

In the beginning of this newfound ability to help, though, our enthusiasm misguided our efforts. We wanted to prevent every bad thing that could possibly happen to our loved ones, especially our children. We were afraid that one single exposure to the wrong thing could turn into a lifelong struggle for them. Our intentions were good, but *fear* was what drove our desire to help.

Fear took it from being charitable to being a very unrealistic and heavy burden, one we put upon ourselves. This fear was what fueled my panic over Hyrum constantly locking himself in his room. But just as I learned not to take Luke's struggles upon myself, I also saw that I couldn't take on my loved one's struggles either. This doesn't mean that I should just let my kids do whatever they want. No, the Savior does not treat us like that. Instead, He teaches unaltered truth with love and clarity and then guides us on how to live within its bounds. He exemplifies the choices that need to be made to obtain lasting happiness. He is a stable place for us to turn to when our hearts are broken—not because He makes us feel comfortable in unrighteous behaviors, or because He prevents all bad from happening in our lives, but because He listens, empathizes, and does everything out of unconditional love.

I can follow Christ's beautiful example and provide an uplifting, stable environment for my loved ones. I may not have all the answers as He does. I may not always say the perfect thing like He can. But if I do my best to listen and talk with them out of love, turning their hearts to Him, then they will know they can come to me again.

My desire to help out of fear really didn't have the potential to help at all, at least not in an effective or lasting way. Why? Because fear turns our focus *away* from the Savior; it shuts us out from accepting His charity, the pure love of Christ. And without charity, our efforts are nothing, for charity is what never fails and endures forever (see Moroni 7:46–47).

Christ's pure love heals. It empowers. His love comforts, guides, directs, and cleanses. As I try to love others, it really is *His love* that I want to fill them with. So helping loved ones is no longer a burden—it's actually a great joy and sacred privilege to guide them to Him, the One whose role it is to take their burdens upon Himself. No matter what the future holds, I feel peace about helping those around us and parenting our children. Luke and I both do because we know what our role is in their life: "We talk of Christ, we rejoice in Christ, we preach of Christ, we prophesy of Christ, and we write according to our prophecies, *that our children may know to what source they may look* for a remission of their sins" (2 Nephi 25:26; emphasis added).

Turn Them to Helpful Resources

Another role I can play in the prevention and healing of this evil perverting the lives of others is to turn them to helpful resources. Throughout the history of the world, God has worked through His children in a variety of ways to uplift the downtrodden. In our day, He guides many to create books, workbooks, workshops, classes, blogs, podcasts, websites, support groups, and more to help the world get out from under lust. He has also inspired therapists to specialize in helping marriages obtain the specific understanding and healing needed from sexual escape and betrayal trauma.

My heart breaks when those who need help purposefully wait to seek out such resources. Years ago, I was one of those people. What makes us see these resources as a last resort? Finances, denial, time, exhaustion, anger, and resentment are some of the reasons I put them off at first. Even my desire to trust completely in the Lord confused me. Do I turn to the Savior and His priesthood, or to a therapist? The answer God helped me discover was "both." As President Oaks taught:

> The use of medical science is not at odds with our prayers of faith and our reliance on priesthood blessings. When a person requested a priesthood blessing, Brigham Young would ask, "Have you used any remedies?" To those who said no because "we wish the Elders to lay hands upon us, and we have faith that we shall be healed," President Young replied: "That is very inconsistent according to my

faith. If we are sick, and ask the Lord to heal us, and to do all for us that is necessary to be done, according to my understanding of the Gospel of salvation, I might as well ask the Lord to cause my wheat and corn to grow, without my plowing the ground and casting in the seed. It appears consistent to me to apply every remedy that comes within the range of my knowledge, and [then] to ask my Father in Heaven . . . to sanctify that application to the healing of my body."[60]

Looking back, Luke and I let our resistance to inspired resources prolong our heartache. We finally decided to do therapy because of Luke's dad. He helped us see how beneficial it could be. If it wasn't for his help in that way, who knows where we would be today? He was also the one who first realized Luke had been misdiagnosed and turned us toward resources to better understand that. I see now that I can be that for others. I can be what he was for us. I can turn those who I know are struggling to helpful resources they may not know about or might be resisting.

Seeing a therapist didn't fix everything. None of the resources we used did. They aren't supposed to, not alone anyway. But they did provide us with multiple sources of understanding and healing, all working synergistically on our wounded marriage. And over time, the Lord really did sanctify the application of them to the healing of our injuries.

Throughout the years, Jesus Christ has worked through many people to help us. Now I want Him to work through me to help others. As wives, we have the opportunity to do His work in this way. Because of the tenderness and knowledge we can gain from this harsh extremity, we have the capacity to truly make a difference in the most authentic way possible. To me, that is comforting, empowering, and oh so sacred.

---

60. Dallin H. Oaks, "Healing the Sick," *Ensign* or *Liahona*, May 2010, 47.

19
I can be humble

COME BACK WITH ME, NOW, TO THE INTRODUCTION OF THIS BOOK when I pleaded with the Lord, "What is to be done? Who of all these parties are right; or, are they all wrong together? If any one of them be right, which is it, and how shall I know it?" (Joseph Smith—History 1:10).

My pleading was interrupted by little tummies needing breakfast, so I took a deep breath and closed my prayer. Moving forward with the hope that "someday, somehow, it will all work out" would have to suffice for now. *Again.*

The next evening, I plopped my exhausted self down on the couch next to Luke after bringing our kids back to their beds for what felt like the hundredth time. I still couldn't get my desperate prayer from the previous morning out of my mind.

Knowing it would be his turn next to bring the kids back when they inevitably got out of bed again, he had pulled up a YouTube video on the TV and paused it before it could start.

"Wait here," he said as he saw a short little head peek out from behind the hall wall. "Don't turn it. I want to show you something."

Curious, I looked up at the screen and saw the title: "Changing the narrative around the addiction story." When he left, his facial expression gave me no clues as to what this change of narrative would be.

"Okay, I think they're finally settled," he said as he came back and sat down next to me. "My dad sent this to me. I haven't watched it yet. I wanted to wait and watch it with you."

It was a TEDx talk at Idaho State University by psychologist Dr. Cameron Staley. He had conducted studies to better understand pornography addiction. What he and his team discovered surprised him. "I was confident," he said, "we would be the first laboratory to find neurological evidence that pornography was an addiction. I was wrong. . . . The brain patterns of our participants looked nothing like those who are addicted to drugs."[61] A correlation they did find, however, was that "people who *believe* they are addicted may then go on to view at higher rates." He went on to say the following:

> The biggest barrier I've come across in helping people change is the belief they are addicted and powerless over their actions. It is the perception that drives the "addiction," not the viewing of sexual images. Unwanted pornography viewing is not a traditional epidemic, but it *is* contagious. Porn problems are spread through language. The very words we've been using to describe the problem—addiction—perpetuate the epidemic. . . . It's time to change the porn story from addiction, isolation, and fear to hope, connection, and understanding.
>
> This is the story I hear from my clients who struggle with porn: They began viewing when they were young because they were curious about sex and simply searching for answers when they weren't even sure of the questions. Later in life, when they were taught pornography was bad, they continued to view in order to manage stress, loneliness, or the beast of all emotions, shame. Viewing helps them feel better temporarily but worse in the long run because they feel ashamed for viewing. It's not just something bad they are doing; shame makes them feel like *they* are bad. Experiencing shame is

---

61. TEDx Talks, "Changing the narrative around the addiction story | Cameron Staley | TEDxIdahoStateUniversity," YouTube video, Dec. 3, 2019, https://youtu.be/mNGg5SMcyhI?si=4MXOFYBgU8xisv4m.

very different from being an addict. Unwanted pornography viewing is an emotional concern, not a sexual problem.[62]

Light bulb after light bulb went off in my mind. I was filled with enlightenment, understanding, and hope as he spoke. He analogized pornography viewing with a symptom, like a cough to a cold. But if viewing is the cough, what's the cold? "The cold," he explained, "is often depression, anxiety, trauma, lack of awareness of emotions, or shame. Fixating on getting rid of the porn cough doesn't treat the cold. Unwanted pornography viewing is a coping strategy for dealing with suffering. Address the cold, and the coping strategy of viewing porn becomes obsolete and goes away." Mindfulness, he went on to detail, was key to addressing the cold.

At some point as he talked, it happened. I'm not exactly sure when, but gradually, familiar dark feelings started to creep their way inside me. Then all at once, I felt angry. All my good thoughts were pushed out, and I was repulsed by the ideas presented in this video. I wanted to turn it off. I wanted to scream and cry and hide all at the same time. I was so furious and didn't slow my mind down to figure out why.

"So . . . what do you think?" Luke said, switching off the TV. He turned nervously, almost sheepishly toward me. He then looked as if he wanted to shout joy from the rooftop but was restraining himself. I could tell he wanted to hear my perspective without it being influenced by his.

"Um . . . yeah, wow! What do you think?" I dodged with a forced smile.

"I think I'm feeling a lot of things," he said, "but mostly good. I . . . I feel . . ." I couldn't tell if he was trying to choose his words carefully or if he was still trying to understand what he was feeling himself. Probably both, I guessed.

This was a gigantic shift from how we had been thinking and living for over ten years—even longer for Luke. He had felt shackled by the chains of addiction for many years before we had even met. Recently, we had discovered the power of mindfulness, but it

---

62. TEDx Talks, "Changing the narrative around the addiction story."

still didn't seem powerful enough to rid our lives of pornography. Something was missing.

"This is the missing piece, Elizabeth! I've experienced the healing effects of the Atonement of Jesus Christ; He has guided me to understand so many useful things, even mindfulness; and He has strengthened me to live and apply those things! But still, I've felt so powerless to let any lasting change stick. It was as if all these years, different people were giving me good and true principles of healing and change, while at the same time saying 'But remember, you *are* still and *will always* be addicted.'"

As he explained his feelings, I remembered the article by President Oaks about the degrees of pornography viewing. In it, he said, "Once we recognize these different levels, we also recognize that not everyone who uses pornography willfully is addicted to it. In fact, most young men and young women who struggle with pornography are not addicted. That is a very important distinction to make—not just for the parents, spouses, and leaders who desire to help *but also for those who struggle with this problem.*"[63]

It seemed that for Luke to realize it wasn't an addiction, and that he had more control than he thought he had, was life-changing in the *best* way possible.

To be honest, it was life-changing for me as well—only in the *worst* way possible.

If he wasn't addicted, and hadn't been this whole time, then that meant he *chose* to betray me, to break our covenants, to make me cry, and to invite such destruction over and over *and over again* into our marriage. He chose. He was in control, and that's what he chose.

I think a part of me always knew that. I mean, I believe in agency. And I knew he was using his agency to give in to temptation. But the addiction narrative is that he, to some extent, gave up a portion of that agency long ago. I couldn't see it as clearly as he could that night, but those two conflicting concepts formed the wall we kept hitting with every new approach we tried.

---

63. Dallin H. Oaks, "Recovering from the Trap of Pornography," *Ensign*, Oct. 2015, 36; emphasis added.

The idea that he was acting as an agent unto himself the whole time was hard for me to swallow. It felt like I was experiencing every single betrayal all over again, all at the same time in that one moment while sitting there with him. I watched as every bit of ground I had gained to heal and trust vanished before my eyes. And in its place was anger.

So much anger.

I hid it as best as I could, but because I felt so justified in it, I didn't want it to go away.

******

After I fed the kids breakfast the next morning and did a morning devotional with them, they ran off to play throughout the house. I envied their innocence. Then I cleaned up the kitchen and quietly slipped into my bathroom to get ready for the day.

I brought my phone with me so I could play some Church-sponsored video clips about pornography. My night of sleep coupled with our devotional must have softened my heart a little bit. My mom's sweet voice echoed in my mind with words she often told me growing up: "Things always look better in the morning." She was right. Instead of wanting to remain in my anger and feelings of betrayal forever, like I had wanted to the previous night, there was a small part of me that still wanted to know what the Lord thought. Was it an addiction? With that question came a spark of hope. Hope for what? I wasn't really sure.

I was standing at my sink, looking into the mirror, toothbrush in hand, when I tapped on one of the videos and heard Elder Rasband's voice:

"Pornography is an affliction."[64]

He went on, but the word *affliction* shook me to my core.

I put down my toothbrush, quickly grabbed my phone, and restarted the video to hear his words once more. I wanted to make sure

---

64. "Individual Overview—Connect and Build Relationships—Addressing Pornography" (video), Gospel Library.

what I thought the Holy Ghost was trying to teach me through them was correct.

"I am the wife of a pornography *addict,*" I told myself as I dragged the stream back to the beginning. That had been my reality—our reality. That was what we were told to help make sense of our suffering, celestial love story. It was supposed to be every answer to the many questions we had about our pain. So for years, we tried our best to apply the treatment for *addiction* to our ever-deepening wounds—his wounds as the addicted and mine as the one his addiction was betraying.

But instead, with each year that passed, it felt more and more like we were applying the wrong medicine. Why was this treatment plan not working? The addiction recovery process is an extremely strong medicine, proven to be effective for other addictions. What were we doing, or not doing, that was wrong?

Never in our wildest imaginings would we have guessed that Luke was just simply *misdiagnosed.*

"Pornography is an affliction," Elder Rasband said again as the video repeated. "An affliction," the Spirit echoed, and then He added, "*Not an addiction.*"

I broke down and began to offer up an intense emotional prayer asking if this was indeed what we were missing after all these years. Was this the *piece* that would finally bring the *peace* and deliverance we both needed and had been seeking?

This knowledge had already provided Luke with the enlightenment and direction he needed, but in my pride and pain, I had resisted it. But as I opened myself up, the Spirit touched me and it became clear: I had a choice to either follow where He was leading or continue to resist in my determination to remain a victim.

After a few moments of honest contemplation, I took a deep breath and made my choice.

And there it was, finally—God's perspective accompanied by complete, unfiltered peace. I left my prayer open for a while, not really saying anything, just crying as I soaked up the light being poured down upon me.

I didn't know what the future would look like exactly, but I knew in that moment that calling Luke's behaviors an addiction was no longer going to lead us down the correct path.

He had an affliction.

And with my surrender came a surprising flood of relief.

20
I can come to be grateful for this extremity

ONE MORNING, YEARS AGO, I WAS MAKING OUR BED. THE SUN WAS shining through the large windows that lined the wall of our bedroom. It was before we had really come to understand how to effectively help others and shortly after I had given birth to Hyrum.

Luke came into the room in tears. It seemed like a scared-about-the-future type of cry. He was in a very stressful graduate school at the time, so I thought that's why he was upset.

"Luke, are you okay? What's wrong?" I asked, putting my hand on his shoulder.

He broke down even more and struggled to get the words out. "I feel so scared for our kids, Elizabeth. Pornography is going to be more easily accessible and commonplace in their world than even when we were young. How will they do it? How can we help them? I feel so defeated. I never want them to go through what we've gone through—what I've gone through."

Luke continued, talking with me about the difficulties of masturbation, which all started for him because of things he overheard on the back of the school bus as a very young boy. We had talked about his long history with this particular sexual struggle before, and it was always heartbreaking. It opened the door to a difficult path of escape for him, one that made him hate himself. But now having a son of our own made the issue of this trial an even more serious discussion. We were afraid about how his curiosity might make things harder for him too.

We hugged, and a conversation I had with a medical doctor years prior came to my mind. I was working as a nurse in a pediatrician's office. I had a question about something she wrote down in a middle-school-aged boy's chart. She clarified it by telling me that part of her patient education was to encourage young boys to masturbate so they could "explore their own sexuality in a safe and healthy way."

Safe? Healthy? My heart sank even further as my mind came back to the present. Luke and I continued to hug, and I realized I didn't only fear the possible lasting effects of our children's own sexual curiosity but also the dangerous information they would inevitably receive from all types of people and places throughout their lives. Clinging to one another, we felt the reality of our kids' future world fall upon us like a dark, looming cloud that even our wall of large windows couldn't brighten.

******

I was getting ready one morning a few days later while my toddler and new baby played on the floor next to me. I was thinking about our conversation, and my stomach dropped as I considered the grasp Satan has on so many through his perversion of intimacy. He has successfully twisted something that is meant to be sacred, bonding, and safe into a weapon of mass destruction in families throughout the world.

With my blow-dryer in hand and my fear escalating, I looked down at my kids and wondered who within my circle of loved ones would be next. Who already is or will be holding dangerous grenades? Who will be caught in the storm of debris and shrapnel that they bring? The realization that it can happen to *anyone* was more than I could handle, and I began to cry.

Soon my mind was brought to the story in the Book of Mormon of Helaman's two thousand stripling warriors. I knew the message was from the Savior by way of the Holy Ghost, but I wasn't sure what the message was exactly. What I did know was that the peace and comfort I so desperately needed lay in their story—the story of those brave and righteous soldiers. So I turned to their account and read, "According to the goodness of God, and to our great astonishment, and also the joy of our whole army, there was not one soul of them who did perish" (Alma 57:25).

Was He saying I didn't need to worry? That no one else I loved would fall prey to this evil and perish at the hand of our spiritual enemy? I prayed and searched to know what He was trying to tell me, but no clarity or further direction came. As is usually the case, I was left to ponder on an impression for much longer than I had anticipated.

******

Many years later, I was making pancakes for my very hungry kids. As was my normal routine, I put a random stream of general conference talks on the TV in the background to soothe my motherhood-induced exhaustion and feed my spirit while I tried to simultaneously meet their every need.

Struggling to listen to the talk over the chorus of requests, I heard Elder Neil L. Andersen's tender voice speak on the different wounds of the soul associated with mortality: "We each understand that difficulties are part of life, but when they come to us personally, they can take our breath away."[65]

I stopped stirring the pancake batter and thought about the lack of oxygen I had suffered through for so many years. I looked down

---

65. Neil L. Andersen, "Wounded," *Ensign* or *Liahona*, Nov. 2018, 84.

at my hands, my arms—my entire body. My eyes filled with tears as I saw my metaphorical wounds of shrapnel either in the process of healing or, amazingly, completely healed.

"How did this happen?" I wondered. "When did this happen?" I knew that our marital battle with sexual escape wasn't completely over. I knew we probably hadn't reached the end of recurrences and were both still in the process of obtaining the change of heart we came to Earth to get. And yet we were living in a state of peace, progression, and connection—connection to each other, to ourselves, and to the Lord.

I started stirring again as I reflected on the recent years that had provided such sweet fruit for our labors. This was after Luke had really started internalizing mindfulness; after I asked him why my pain was not enough, which led to our Recovery Nights; after he and I found the balance of using the psychological tools gained from therapy and the spiritual power available through our covenants; after we started reaching out to help others who suffered from the wounds we knew all too well; and after we learned that Luke was not addicted. It was after many years of the Lord providing a lot of little answers—a series of answers,[66] line upon line—that we finally felt *consistently* strengthened through the power of Jesus Christ to act as agents and impact the circumstances of our marriage.

Then Elder Andersen's voice penetrated my trance of awe: "When telling the miraculous story of Helaman's 2,060 young soldiers, we love this scripture: 'According to the goodness of God, and to our great astonishment, and also the joy of our whole army, there was not one soul of them who did perish.'"

The Spirit touched me as I recalled my plea to receive comfort and understanding from this very story and this very verse years prior. I listened intently as he went on:

> But the sentence continues: "And neither was there one soul among them who had not received many wounds." Each one of the 2,060

---

66. True Millennial, "How to Share the Gospel on Social Media // Interview with Elder Bednar," YouTube video, Aug. 18, 2024, https://youtu.be/SrNnKfKXv-U?si=gR5QJH8CNuXmVn34.

received many wounds, and each one of us will be wounded in the battle of life, whether physically, spiritually, or both.

Never give up—however deep the wounds of your soul, whatever their source, wherever or whenever they happen, and however short or long they persist, you are not meant to perish spiritually. You are meant to survive spiritually and blossom in your faith and trust in God. . . . In the crucible of earthly trials, patiently move forward, and the Savior's healing power will bring you light, understanding, peace, and hope.[67]

My loved ones *will* fall prey to the evils of Satan, either sexual escapes or some other evil. They *will* be wounded in the war over the hearts of the children of men. But like Helaman's warriors and like Luke and I, *they will not perish spiritually* if they turn to the Savior and allow Him to heal their many wounds.

Like us, they too can discover that "no pain that we suffer, no trial that we experience is wasted. It ministers to our education, to the development of such qualities as patience, faith, fortitude and humility. All that we suffer and all that we endure, especially when we endure it patiently, builds up our characters, purifies our hearts, expands our souls, and makes us more tender and charitable, more worthy to be called the children of God. . . . It is through sorrow and suffering, toil and tribulation, that we gain the education that we come here to acquire."[68]

As I reflected in the calm and quiet that cooked pancakes bring to our household, I felt grateful for the education our marriage had been for me. The process of seeking out righteousness and healing with an afflicted yet humble spouse has refined me in unexpected ways—unexpected to me but not to my Heavenly Father or to His Son, Jesus Christ. They've always seen the person I was capable of becoming. They took the difficult path mortality presented me with and showed me how to use it for my eternal benefit.

With enlightenment still flowing, I leaned against the counter to start eating my own pancake. My mind was piecing it all together.

---

67. Neil L. Andersen, "Wounded," 84–85.
68. Orson F. Whitney, quoted in Spencer W. Kimball, *Faith Precedes the Miracle* (Deseret Book, 1972), 98.

Truly, my Liberty Jail experience really had been built into a temple, just like President Holland said it could be, which made me think about a story told by Sister Linda S. Reeves:

> Almost three years ago a devastating fire gutted the interior of the beloved, historic tabernacle in Provo, Utah. Its loss was deemed a great tragedy by both the community and Church members. Many wondered, "Why did the Lord let this happen? Surely He could have prevented the fire or stopped its destruction."
>
> Ten months later . . . there was an audible gasp when President Thomas S. Monson announced that the nearly destroyed tabernacle was to become a holy temple—a house of the Lord! Suddenly we could see what the Lord had always known! He didn't cause the fire, but He allowed the fire to strip away the interior. He saw the tabernacle as a magnificent temple—a permanent home for making sacred, eternal covenants.
>
> My dear sisters, the Lord allows us to be tried and tested, sometimes to our maximum capacity. We have seen the lives of loved ones—and maybe our own—figuratively burned to the ground and have wondered why a loving and caring Heavenly Father would allow such things to happen. But He does not leave us in the ashes; He stands with open arms, eagerly inviting us to come to Him. He is building our lives into magnificent temples where His Spirit can dwell eternally.[69]

Considering all that I've faced to strip away my interior, and even knowing that my days of painful refinement have not come to an end, I have to ask myself: Was it worth it?

Years ago my husband and I knelt across an altar, tenderly holding each other's hands. We gazed into one another's eyes with excitement for the beautiful days ahead. In our real but somewhat naive love, we made sacred promises to each other and to God. But if I knew then what our marriage would go through, would I still have said yes?

Yes. Unequivocally yes.

Enduring this with Luke and the Lord, our Master who truly never did leave us in this field alone, has sanctified our marriage.

---

69. Linda S. Reeves, "Claim the Blessings of Your Covenants," *Ensign* or *Liahona*, Nov. 2013, 119.

Through our hardship, we have been blessed with a relationship that is so beautiful—so full of joy, unselfish love, and communication—that I already feel to say to my Heavenly Father, "Was that *all* that was required?"[70]

Amazingly, our reward for binding ourselves to Him and to each other by taking His yoke upon us doesn't end with the blessings received in this life. There is so much more! And when that day comes and we stand face-to-face with the One who carried us through, "what will it matter, dear sisters, what we suffered here if, in the end, those trials are the very things which qualify us for eternal life and exaltation in the kingdom of God with our Father and Savior?"[71]

Perhaps Luke and I could have learned these lessons in other ways, so this trial and suffering should not be sought after. But this was our life. This is our life. *Embracing* this extremity as our refiner's fire, our sacred education, *allows it to be God's opportunity*—His opportunity to teach us, to purify us, and to guide us in living a mortal experience filled with peace, happiness, growth, and connection. And if we continue to let Him, it's the very extremity He can use to qualify us for a life hereafter beyond anything we can imagine.

So hold on your way and God's power will remain with you now and into the eternities. That is His promise to us all. It's a promise that can enable you to understand what you are feeling, strengthen you to identify what you need, and empower you to act in the ways you can to impact your circumstances for your eternal gain and that of your family.

Your extremity *is* God's opportunity. Will you let it be?

---

70. Linda S. Reeves, "Worthy of Our Promised Blessings," *Ensign* or *Liahona*, Nov. 2015, 11.
71. Linda S. Reeves, "Worthy of Our Promised Blessings," 11.

About the Author

The author lives in North Carolina with her husband and five kids. Strengthened by her deep faith and covenants, she wrote *God's Opportunity*, her first book, as a heartfelt exploration of marital healing. Drawing on personal experiences applying the gospel of Jesus Christ to her own marriage, she offers a hopeful path to couples who have been afflicted by pornography—a path toward rebuilding their love, one chapter at a time.